THE GRAPEVINE
Quick and Tasty Cookbook

BY
LIZ BYRSKI & PETER HOLLAND

> When there is no more cookery in the world, there will be no more letters, no quick and lofty intelligence, no more pleasant easy relationships: no more social unity.
>
> Careme

FREMANTLE ARTS CENTRE PRESS

Illustrations by Yvette Ricciardello

Cover photograph by Victor France,
with thanks to Granitas Café, South Fremantle.

First published 1996 by
FREMANTLE ARTS CENTRE PRESS
193 South Terrace (PO Box 320), South Fremantle
Western Australia 6162
in association with
the Australian Broadcasting Corporation.

Copyright compilation © Liz Byrski & Peter Holland, 1996.
Copyright individual recipes © individual contributors, 1996
(unless otherwise noted).

This book is copyright. Apart from any fair dealing for the purpose of private study, research, criticism or review, as permitted under the Copyright Act, no part may be reproduced by any process without written permission. Enquiries should be made to the publisher.

Consulting Editor B R Coffey.
Designed by John Douglass.
Production coordinator Linda Martin.

Typeset by Fremantle Arts Centre Press
and printed by South China Printing Company.

National Library of Australia
Cataloguing-in-publication data

The grapevine quick and tasty cookbook.

ISBN 1 86368 174 4.

1. Cookery. I. Byrski, Liz. II. Holland, Peter, 1944 - .

641.5

The State of Western Australia has made an investment in this project through the Department for the Arts.

Contents

Introduction	5
Soup	7
Salads and Dressings	18
Vegetarian Dishes	26
Meat and Poultry	37
Fish and Seafood	50
Pasta and Rice Dishes	57
Desserts	66
Cakes, Biscuits, Bread	75
Pickles, Preserves, Beverages	85
'What's Cooking'	92
Index	94

We may live without poetry, music and art;
We may live without conscience, and live without heart;
We may live without friends; we may live without books;
But civilised man cannot live without cooks.
He may live without books — what is knowledge but grieving?
He may live without hope — what is hope without deceiving
He may live without love — what is passion without pining?
But where is the man that can live without dining?

Owen Meredith, *Lucile*. Pt. 1. Canot 11.

INTRODUCTION

Welcome to *The Grapevine Quick and Tasty Cookbook*.

The idea for the book came from the Grapevine radio program which first went to air in February 1995. It began its life as a 'swap meet' of the airwaves but soon became much more than that. The Grapevine developed a life of its own as a wide-ranging and effective community network through which people could find not only the things they needed, but get in touch with old friends and make new ones, ask for help or volunteer it, and track down information from the trivial to the essential. Within a few months we were overwhelmed by the response of the 720 audience and the way in which the program seemed to act as a catalyst for community involvement, and a channel through which 'Grapies' could direct their goodwill, energy and desire to play an active role in their community.

When the program was extended in 1996 we decided to broadcast a recipe each day. Neither of us is a good or enthusiastic cook so we asked Grapies to send us their favourite quick and easy recipes which even 'cookaphobes' like us could manage. We soon had more recipes than we could use and it seemed a good idea to combine the pick of them in a book which, as well as being a useful publication, might also to help to raise funds for a good cause.

A number of organisations applied to be the recipients of the profits and all were worthy bodies whom we would have loved to be able to support. Picking one organisation was really difficult but finally we chose CanTeen, the Australian Teenage Cancer Patients Society, a national support network for teenagers with cancer and their adolescent brothers and sisters.

CanTeen is based on the belief that young people, through talking and meeting with one another, are better able to cope with the uncertainty of cancer and the trauma associated with treatment, hospitalisation and possible death. Many of us here at 720 have met some of those young people and were impressed by their wisdom and courage. We hope we will sell enough of these books to make a useful contribution to their funds.

We have not tested all the recipes in the book, relying rather on the wisdom of the Grapevine to ensure that what courage. We hope we will sell enough of these books to make a useful contribution to their funds.

We have not tested all the recipes in the book, relying rather on the wisdom of the Grapevine to ensure that what we were sent really worked. We have tried some of them, as have other 720 staff members and all reported successes. There was only one exception: the 'Peter-Proof Chocolate Cake' on page 83. Peter had a go at this one and the result was not something we wish to remember. Since then we have tested the recipe and now realise that while the recipe is fine Holland is best kept out of the kitchen.

It simply was not possible to publish all the recipes and it was hard to decide which to include and which to leave out. Many thanks to the hundreds of listeners who generously sent us their recipes, and special thanks to those who have allowed them to be used in this book.

The book would not have come together without the hard work of a number of people. 720s Marketing Manager, Sharron Booth, not only coordinated the project (she actually made it happen) but prepared and typed many of the recipes. Our tireless Administrative Officer, Leonie Nicholls, typed and sorted recipes and answered numerous enquiries from listeners. 720 producer Bev East also helped out with typing, as did Di Yarrall. Lis Smyth kindly provided the quotations on food which appear throughout the book. Our thanks go to all of them.

We are grateful, too, to Fremantle Arts Centre Press for making a leap of faith and publishing the book.

No radio program makes it into the public arena without a stalwart production crew and the Grapevine is no exception. Very special thanks go to Co-presenter Karen Buck, Producer Rosemary Greenham, Technical Producer John Woodley, and Shirley Lowrie from the ABC Sound Library who unfailingly manages to come up with the goods to satisfy Grapies' musical requests.

And, of course, our thanks to Grapies everywhere for making the Grapevine into much more than just a radio program.

We hope you will enjoy trying the recipes which Grapies have perfected. And don't forget to join us on the Grapevine — Monday to Friday on ABC Radio 720 6WF.

Liz Byrski
Peter Holland

Soup

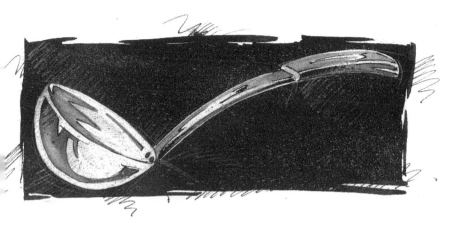

PK'S APPLE AND PUMPKIN SOUP

1 onion, chopped
2½ cms fresh ginger, grated
3 medium apples, cored & diced
½ butternut pumpkin, peeled & diced
5 cms lemon rind
1 tsp mustard

1 tsp turmeric
1 tsp cumin
1 tsp coriander
2 cups chicken stock
½ tsp nutmeg
½ cup skim milk

Put onion and ginger into a pan with 2 tbs water. Cover and cook over medium heat for 2-3 minutes. Add pumpkin and apple and cook, covered, for a further 3 minutes. Add the lemon peel, spices except nutmeg, and chicken stock.

Bring to the boil and simmer for about 20 minutes, or until pumpkin is tender enough to mash. Puree soup in a food processor.

Return to pan and add skim milk and nutmeg. Reheat but do not boil.

Not only do I enjoy making apple and pumpkin soup, it's big on low-fat ingredients — a feature I find especially attractive.

From Peter Kennedy, 720 6WF morning presenter.

Of soup and love, the first is best.
Old Spanish proverb.

COMPOST SOUP

Leftover vegetables in refrigerator
1 large onion, chopped
2 potatoes, peeled & diced
$2/_3$ cup red lentils
1 tbs parsley flakes
4 cups chicken stock

Dice leftover vegetables and add to stockpot with all other ingredients.

Bring to the boil, then lower the heat and simmer for about an hour, until the vegetables are tender. Season to taste.

I always make this soup at the end of the week, just before I go out to buy the next week's supplies.

From Jean Caley of Samson.

CARROT AND CAULIFLOWER SOUP

500 gms fresh carrots
375 gms cauliflower
1 onion
1 clove garlic
1 litre vegetable stock
1 tbs oil

Chop all vegetables into small pieces and fry in oil for 2 minutes. Add stock, bring to boil and simmer until vegetables are tender enough to mash.

Blend in a food processor, reheat and serve with croutons.

From Charles Coote of Bedford.

CALDO VERDE

500 gms peeled potatoes
4 tsp olive oil
250 gms cabbage leaves, finely shredded
Few slices of chorizo sausage or spicy salami
1 litre water, salted
1 onion, chopped
Ground black pepper

Boil the potatoes in the salted water until they are soft enough to mash. Transfer the potatoes to a bowl and save the water. Mash, and return them to the saucepan with the water.

Add the oil, onion, chorizo and cabbage and boil for 3-4 minutes. Season and serve very hot.

Caldo Verde is a Portuguese recipe.

From Brough McLead of Canning Bridge.

BANANA CURRY SOUP

160 gms onion, finely chopped
50 gms butter
2 tsp curry powder
2 tsp flour
450 gms ripe bananas

30 mls lemon juice
30 mls water
1200 mls chicken stock
90 mls double cream

Sweat onion in butter until soft, not coloured. Add curry powder and flour, and fry. Skin bananas, put in blender with lemon juice and water. Blend to puree. Add to onions, add stock and bring to the boil. Season to taste and simmer for 15 minutes.

Serve either hot or chilled. Add double cream to taste.

From Kay Owen of Edgewater.

BUTTERNUT PUMPKIN MICROWAVE SOUP

1 butternut pumpkin
1 tsp dried parsley

1 tsp chives
Salt, pepper to taste

Wipe the pumpkin clean, then place it whole in the microwave. Cook on High for approximately 12 minutes. Allow to cool sufficiently to enable you to skin and de-seed the pumpkin. Cut into small pieces.

Pop them into a 2 litre microwave jug. Gradually add 3-4 cups water, more if a thinner soup is desired. Add dried parsley and chives. Blend with electric wand or fork. Reheat and serve.

From Sylvia Somerville of Kelmscott.

VICHYSSOISE

4 cups chicken stock
4 medium potatoes, peeled & chopped
3 medium onions, chopped
3 leeks, sliced
1 tbs orange rind

2 tsp marjoram
2 tbs parsley
150 mls low-fat yoghurt
Pepper to taste

Place chicken stock into large pan and bring to boil. Add potatoes, onions, leeks and orange rind and simmer for 20 minutes. Cool a little, then blend.

Add other ingredients and serve. It can also be served chilled.

From Margaret Graham of Stoneville and reproduced with kind permission from Penguin Books, publishers of Julie Stafford's Taste Of Life.

CHINESE CHICKEN AND CORN SOUP

Chicken pieces or breasts
1 can whole corn kernels
1 can creamed corn

Garlic, fresh ginger
Spring onions
Chicken stock powder

Coarsely chop and simmer the chicken. Add corn kernels, creamed corn, stock powder and plenty of ginger and garlic. Bring to the boil. Add coarsely chopped spring onions and serve.

We received a couple of variations of this much-loved favourite. Some suggested adding ham strips and a few drops of sesame oil.

From Leonie of Langford and Jean of Rossmoyne.

BETH'S WILD RICE AND SPINACH SOUP

$2/3$ cup wild rice
4 cups vegetable broth/stock
1 cup finely chopped onions
1 small garlic clove
2 tbs butter/oil
2 pkts frozen spinach

$1/2$ cup light cream
1 tsp curry powder
1 tsp salt
$1/4$ tsp pepper
Lemon slices to garnish

Wash wild rice thoroughly in hot tap-water, then drain. Place into saucepan with 2½ cups vegetable broth and bring to the boil. Simmer for 35-40 minutes.

Saute onions and garlic in butter until tender. Add spinach and remaining broth, simmer for approximately 10 minutes until spinach is cooked. Place in blender and puree until smooth.

Return to saucepan and add the remaining ingredients, plus cooked rice and any leftover broth not absorbed by the rice.

Serve with a twist of lemon.

From Sally Gatt-Lodding of Victoria Park.

CARROT AND CORIANDER SOUP

2 tsp coriander
500 gms carrots
2 small onions

1 litre chicken stock
1 tbs oil/butter

Dice carrots and onions. Cook in oil for 5 minutes. Pour in stock and bring to boil. Simmer for approximately 40 minutes. Add coriander and simmer for 5 minutes. Blend in food processor, reheat and serve.

From Pauline Taylor from Brentwood.

EGG SOUP

2 tbs oil
2 tbs flour
¼ tsp caraway seeds
2 cups water
1 bay leaf

6 peppercorns
1 tbs white vinegar
2 tbs sour cream
2 eggs
1 tsp paprika

Heat oil in saucepan. Add caraway seeds and flour. Stir on a low heat until lightly browned. Add paprika, then water. Stir to prevent lumps. Add bay leaf, peppercorns and salt. Bring to the boil. While stirring, slowly add lightly beaten eggs. Add vinegar and sour cream.

From Edith Thomas of Kallaroo.

ABBUNDANZA SOUP

1 red capsicum
1 zucchini
2 onions
2 carrots
2 sticks celery

1 large can tomatoes
1 small can kidney beans
Dried basil
Parmesan cheese
Garlic

Chop vegetables. Boil all ingredients except beans and cheese, until soft.

Add beans and season with salt and pepper. Heat through and serve sprinkled with parmesan cheese.

From Leonie of Langford.

Soup and fish explain half the emotions of life.
Sydney Smith.

NANNA TRAWINSKI'S CABBAGE SOUP

1 pack pork soup bones
1 tsp freshly cracked black pepper
Pinch salt
3-4 bay leaves
3-4 litres water
$1/2$ cabbage

1 carrot
2-3 small tomatoes
1 large onion
1 tbs butter
1 cup milk/cream
1 tbs cornflour

Make soup stock with bones, pepper, salt, bay leaves and water. Cook slowly for 2-3 hours, until the meat comes off the bones easily. Strain and reserve some of the meat to add to the soup before serving.

Shred cabbage, slice carrot and tomatoes. Dice onion and fry gently in butter until golden. Add all vegetables to the stock and cook slowly for 1 hour.

Thicken with a little cornflour added to milk/cream and bring back to the boil.

From Jean Trawinski of Calista.

MUM'S GREEN SOUP

Potatoes boiled in water or stock
2-3 sticks celery, sliced
1 onion, chopped (or shallots)
2 rashers bacon, finely chopped

Tasty cheese, grated
Milk
Salt

Use about as many potatoes as you would when serving the family mashed potato.

Put everything in a pot and boil until the potatoes are ready to mash. Remove them from pot and mash or whisk well. Add a dob of butter and milk. Beat until smooth and throw it back in the pot with other ingredients. Reheat. If too thick, add more milk.

Serve with grated cheese.

From Jenny of Doubleview.

POTATO AND LAMB SOUP

1 tbs oil
1 kg lamb shanks, cut in 3
1 onion, chopped
2 cloves garlic, crushed
2 carrots, chopped
2 sticks celery, chopped
810 gms canned tomatoes

$1\frac{1}{2}$ litres water
3 tsp beef stock powder
5 large potatoes, chopped
2 medium zucchini, diced
2 tbs tomato paste
2 tbs chopped basil
$\frac{1}{2}$ tsp sugar

Heat oil, add shanks and brown all over. Remove from pan. Add onion, garlic, carrots and celery to pan and cook, stirring, until onion is soft. Return shanks to pan, add undrained chopped tomatoes. Add water and stock powder. Simmer, covered, for approximately 1 hour, or until lamb is tender.

Remove meat from shanks and chop roughly. Discard bones. Bring soup to the boil in the pan. Add chopped meat, potatoes, zucchini, tomato paste, basil and sugar.

Simmer uncovered for about 10 minutes, or until potatoes are tender.

From Catherine McIntosh of Ongerup.

COLD SHANNON SOUP

2 x 430 ml cans beef consomme
400 mls vegetable juice
400 mls tomato juice
Tabasco to taste
120 mls thickened cream

Ensure consomme and juices are chilled for at least 12 hours prior to using.

Put consomme into a large mixing bowl. Add juices and Tabasco and whisk until thoroughly blended. Stir in cream and chill again, until just set.

Serve with a wedge of lemon, a teaspoon of whipped cream and a sprinkling of nutmeg.

From Mary of Manning.

R.F.T'S 5-DAY SOUP

2 tbs soy sauce
2 tbs Worcestershire sauce
1 dsp mixed herbs
1 dsp granulated garlic
1 dsp Anchor Soup Mix
1 dsp pearl barley
1 pkt instant soup
Bacon bones
2 carrots
2 potatoes
2 onions
1 leek
stock cube
5 litres water

Put soy, Worcestershire, herbs, garlic, soup mix, barley, bones and water in a large pot. Bring to the boil and add chopped vegetables,stock cube and instant soup. Simmer for at least 5 hours.

15 minutes before serving, add some chopped parsley.

This should last 2 people about 5 days.

From Ray Twist of Lesmurdie.

I believe I once considerably scandalised her by declaring that clear soup was a more important factor than a clear conscience.

Saki.

LYNDA'S LOVELY LETTUCE SOUP

1 whole lettuce, washed and chopped
1 leek or bunch spring onions, chopped
1 heaped tbs chicken stock powder
1/2 tsp dried tarragon, or herbs to your taste
1 onion, finely diced
1 cup frozen or fresh peas
2 litres water

Saute onions in a little oil until soft. Add all vegetables, steam until wilted. Add stock powder, tarragon and water. Simmer 20 minutes, cool slightly, then blend in food processor.

From Lynda of Balcatta.

LENTIL SOUP

1 cup brown lentils
1 carrot
1 potato
1 onion, chopped
Bacon pieces
1 1/2 litres soup stock
1 stick celery

Braise bacon in saucepan. Add chopped vegetables, lentils and stock and simmer until tender. This should take about 30 minutes.

From Pippa of Fremantle.

TOMATO AND YOGHURT SOUP

2 x 397 gm cans tomatoes
2 cloves garlic, crushed
Juice 1 lemon
1 tbs sugar
1 tbs Worcestershire sauce
400 mls low-fat yoghurt
Salt, pepper

Put tomatoes, including juice, in a blender with garlic, lemon juice, sugar and Worcestershire sauce. Blend for approximately 3 minutes until smooth. Stir in yoghurt and add salt and pepper to taste.

Chill for at least 4 hours.

From Kay Owen of Edgewater.

CHILLED ROCKMELON SOUP

1 very ripe rockmelon
1 dsp sweet Malaysian curry powder
Cream or yoghurt

Slice rockmelon and make some melon balls for garnish. Blend the rest of the rockmelon in a food processor until smooth, but not liquid. Add curry powder to taste. Add enough cream to make a smooth soup.

Serve chilled and garnished with melon balls and mint sprigs.

From Deborah Watt of Dianella.

TOMATO AND SEAFOOD SOUP

440 gms can tomato soup
30 gms butter/margarine
1 onion
1 clove garlic
1 tbs sherry
$1/2$ cup water
$1/2$ cup sour cream
200 gms can crab meat
1 tbs chopped chives

Fry onion and garlic in butter until transparent. Add sour cream, crab, soup and water. Mix thoroughly until soup is smooth. Stir until hot, not boiling. Stir in chives and sherry just prior to serving.

From Sue of Greenwood.

SUMMER SOUP

2 large cups pineapple juice, chilled
2 large cups tomato juice, chilled
Small carton cream

Combine pineapple and tomato juice thoroughly. Swirl the cream over the top of the soup and serve immediately.

From Ailsa of Dunsborough.

CHRISTINA'S THAI CHICKEN AND RICE SOUP WITH CORIANDER.

1 chicken breast
100 gms jasmine rice
3 tbs fish sauce
1 dsp minced garlic
1 dsp chopped or grated ginger
$1/3$ tsp white pepper
6 small spring onions
Plenty of coriander
2 small red chillies

Wash and skin the chicken breast and cut into very small pieces. Wash the rice and then cook in about 1 litre water. Cook until just tender, don't allow it to get really soft. Do not drain; the water will be part of the soup.

In a non-stick pan, cook the garlic and ginger gently for a few minutes. Add the chopped chicken and cook gently for about 5 minutes. Add white pepper. Add the fish sauce and simmer gently for a couple more minutes. Add the chicken mixture to the rice in its water and stir through. Simmer gently for about 1 minute.

Put the soup into deep bowls and sprinkle with finely chopped spring onions (the green bits are especially good), and finely chopped chillies.

Finally, sprinkle liberally with roughly chopped coriander, and serve.

This quantity makes enough for 2 people. If there are leftovers you can use them up by adding more water to the rice and chicken mix, and more fish sauce to taste.

This recipe was given to me by my friend Christina. I love it because it's economical and low fat, and because it's so delicious that everyone for whom I've served it really loves it. It's satisfying enough to be a meal in itself. I think the Thais use it as a breakfast soup; I love it any time of day.

From Liz Byrski, 720 6WF Grapevine presenter.

SALADS & DRESSINGS

PUMPKIN AND MUSTARD SALAD

250 gms pumpkin, peeled and sliced
1/4 green capsicum, chopped
1 tsp wholegrain mustard
1/2 tsp ground cumin
1/4 tsp powdered ginger
150 mls yoghurt

Steam pumpkin and keep warm. Combine the rest of the ingredients and pour over the pumpkin. Serve on its own or with cooked pasta.

From Rosemary of Booragoon.

SPINACH SALAD

1 bunch spinach/young silverbeet
1 pear, cored and sliced thinly
100-150 gms chopped ham
1/2 red capsicum, sliced
60 gms toasted pine nuts

Shred spinach and thinly slice capsicum. Combine all ingredients and serve with a creamy salad dressing.

From Rosemary of Booragoon.

CHARLIE'S SUMMER SALAD

Lettuce, shredded
Onion, sliced
Capsicum, sliced
Cucumber, sliced
1 small tin crushed pineapple
Carrot, grated
Celery, finely chopped
Cherry tomatoes
2 hard-boiled eggs

Combine all salad vegetables and chill well. Immediately before serving, fold the chilled crushed pineapple gently through the salad and place sliced and chilled hard-boiled eggs on top. Serve with barbecued fish or chicken.

I got this recipe from Charlie of Wild Geese International, a group of retired servicemen and women. Charlie was a cook in the navy and shared this recipe with me over the CB radio.

From Michelle of Kelmscott.

SILVERBEET SALAD

Silverbeet leaves, shredded
Red capsicum, chopped
Cooked macaroni

Toss together equal amounts of above ingredients. Dress with a garlicky vinaigrette.

From Cas Brown of City Beach.

COPPER PENNY SALAD

2 kgs carrots, sliced into rings
2 onions, sliced into rings
1 capsicum, sliced
1 cup celery, sliced
425 gm can tomato soup
$1/3$ cup oil
$3/4$ cup cider vinegar
$1/2$ cup sugar
1 tsp French mustard
1 tsp Worcestershire sauce

Put all ingredients together and mix. Leave for 24 hours before using.

From Audrey Goldsworthy of Rockingham.

During suppers which Louis XIV would have with the princesses and ladies at Marly, it sometimes happened that the King, who was very dexterous, amused himself by throwing little rolls of bread at the ladies and allowed all of them to throw them at him ... it is said that Mlle de Vautois, lady-in-waiting to the Princess de Conti, the King's daughter, threw her salad at him, fully seasoned.

Duke of Luynes.

MEDITERRANEAN PASTA SALAD

250 gms penne pasta
2 tbs olive oil
1 small red capsicum, sliced
1 small green capsicum, sliced
90 gms peperoni, skinned & julienned
1 cup zucchini, coarsely shredded
1 tomato, chopped
$3/4$ cup grated cheddar
$3/4$ cup grated cheddar or provolone cheese
$1/2$ cup chopped parsley
$1/2$ cup black olives
$1/3$ cup chopped onion

Cook pasta in boiling, salted water until 'al dente'. Drain and rinse under cold running water. Place in a large bowl, add oil and toss well. Add other ingredients and lightly toss to mix. Serve with a vinaigrette dressing.

From Fay Littely of Hamersley.

SILVERBEET SALAD No. 2

5 young silverbeet leaves, shredded
1 carrot, grated
1 apple, finely chopped
1 cup bean shoots
$1/2$ cup sultanas
Sesame seeds

Toss all ingredients except sesame seeds together and mix well. Dress with commercial or homemade French dressing and sprinkle with sesame seeds.

From Cas Brown of City Beach.

RENEE'S DEFINITIVE CAESAR SALAD

1 large or 2 small Cos (Romain) lettuce well chilled, washed and dried
4 large anchovies, very finely sliced
2 cloves garlic
¼ cup white wine vinegar
½ cup extra virgin olive oil — no other
2 tbs grated parmesan cheese
1 raw egg
Juice 1 lemon
1 tsp Worcestershire sauce
½ tsp dried mustard or 1 tsp seeded mustard
Salt, black pepper to taste
1 cup garlic croutons (see recipe below)

Roughly chop or crush one of the garlic cloves and place it in the oil, stir and allow to stand for 30 minutes. Strain. Cut the other garlic clove in half, and rub a wooden bowl thoroughly with the cut side. Tear lettuce into bite-sized pieces and put into the bowl.

Break egg over the lettuce, and pour lemon juice over the egg. Toss until egg is thoroughly distributed through the lettuce. Add anchovies, mustard, salt, pepper, Worcestershire sauce, vinegar and strained garlic oil, and toss again. Top with cheese and garlic croutons and serve immediately.

Garlic croutons: Cut crusts off 4-5 slices bread. Cube bread and place in bowl. Add 1-2 cloves crushed garlic, 1 tbs parmesan cheese, salt, pepper and 1-2 tbs olive oil. Toss. Spread on non-stick baking sheet and bake for 9 minutes. Turn halfway through. Cool before using.

From Renee of Scarborough.

QUICK SUMMER SALAD

125 gms tuna in brine
½ cup quick-cook brown rice
Handful cashews/peanuts
1 tbs soy sauce
1 stick celery, chopped

Place rice in 1 cup of warm water and leave in the fridge, preferably overnight. Drain tuna and stir into the cooked rice. Add the celery and stir in soy sauce, making sure all rice is coated. Stir through the nuts and serve.

From Margaret Hamilton of Perth.

SEAFOOD SALAD

1 large avocado	1/2 head lettuce
300 gms seafood salad cuts	2/3 cup mayonnaise
12 prawns	Tomato sauce
1/2 bunch shallots	Cracked pepper

Combine the mayonnaise and tomato sauce. Season with a generous quantity of cracked pepper. Chop everything else and combine with mayonnaise mixture. Add lemon juice to taste.

Several variations of the seafood salad were received. This is from Janette of Sorrento.

*Serenely full, the epicure would say,
Fate cannot harm me, I have dined today.*

Sydney Smith, *Receipt for a Salad.*

PAT'S NOODLE SALAD

1/2 Chinese cabbage	1/3 cup slivered almonds
1 pkt cooked 2-Minute Noodles	1/4 cup sunflower seeds
1 cup frozen peas, cooked	

Shred cabbage, add peas, almonds, sunflower seeds and chopped noodles.

Other vegetables such as shallots, grated carrot and sweet corn can be added.

Dressing: Mix the sachet of flavouring from the noodles with 2 tbs sugar, 3 tbs vinegar and 1/4 cup olive oil. Mix well and add to salad just before serving.

From Jenny Sleep of Wilson.

CAESAR POTATO SALAD

10-12 gourmet potatoes
1 egg
¼ cup Italian dressing
¼ cup grated cheese
1 tbs Worcestershire sauce
2 tsp mustard
Salt
4 pitted olives

Cook potatoes, rinse, drain and cool. Chop or dice potatoes. Slice pitted olives. Combine egg, dressing, cheese, Worcestershire sauce and mustard.

Mix thoroughly and season to taste. Mix olives and potatoes, and pour dressing over. Toss and serve well chilled.

From Barbara Hanney of Sorrento.

VERITY'S CHILLI CHICKEN SALAD

2 chicken breasts
2 spring onions, finely chopped
2 tbs fresh coriander, chopped
2 stalks lemongrass (just finely slice the white bits)
2 tbs fresh mint, chopped
2 tbs onion, finely sliced

Dressing:
2 tbs fish sauce
2 tbs lime or lemon juice
1 tsp sugar
2 red chillies, finely sliced

Mix all dressing ingredients together and let sugar dissolve. Skin chicken and then grill or microwave until just cooked, then shred or dice.

Combine all salad items together in a bowl, then mix chicken, dressing and salad together. It can be stretched further with finely sliced, raw red cabbage or a couple of handfuls of 'yuppie' mixed salad greens.

From Verity James, 720 6WF morning presenter.

CONTINENTAL TUNA SALAD

275 gms pasta spirals, Vegeroni preferred
100 gms French beans, halved
Large can 4-Bean Mix
Fresh parsley, chopped
60 mls low-fat French dressing
185 gm can tuna in brine
Black pepper to taste

Add pasta to boiling water and cook. Just before it's ready, add beans.

Drain and rinse immediately in very cold water. Combine all ingredients, season to taste. Serve chilled.

From Susan of Applecross.

There's no sauce in the world like hunger.
Cerventes, Don Quixote.

MARSHMALLOW SALAD

2 pkts marshmallows
425 gm tin 2-fruits, well drained
1 tin pineapple pieces
2 bananas
2 oranges
2 eggs
$1/4$ cup vinegar
$1/2$ cup sugar
2 tbs butter/margarine
1 carton cream

Place marshmallows and fruit in a bowl and combine thoroughly.

Beat the eggs, vinegar and sugar over medium heat until it thickens. Add butter and stir well. Remove from heat and allow to cool. Whip cream and add to egg mixture.

Combine all ingredients and mix well. Chill for 24 hours.

From Teresa Farrell of Mount Hawthorn.

MARGARET'S MAYONNAISE

1 can sweetened condensed milk
2 eggs
2 tsp dry mustard
2 tsp salt
1 cup vinegar
$\frac{1}{2}$ cup salad oil

Blend condensed milk eggs, salt and mustard. Gradually add vinegar, then add oil very gradually.

Salt and mustard can be varied according to taste. This quantity makes 2 medium-sized jars and will keep in the fridge forever.

From Margaret Mitchell.

HERB VINAIGRETTE

1 cup light olive oil
1 tsp Dijon mustard
1 clove garlic
2 tbs wine vinegar
2 tbs fresh herbs: dill, basil, parsley etc.

Blend all ingredients in food processor. Bottle and chill before serving.

From Irene of Booragoon.

SOUR CREAM DRESSING

1 small carton light sour cream
1 medium white onion, finely chopped
Juice of 1 orange

Mix all ingredients and allow to stand, preferably for $\frac{1}{2}$ - 1 day before use, to allow the onion flavour to infuse. Terrific for any salad; even for coleslaw.

From Kathryn Kuijpers of Duncraig.

VEGETARIAN DISHES

PAN HAGGERTY

Onion, finely chopped
Tomatoes, sliced
Grated cheese
A little margarine
Raw potatoes, sliced into thin circles (to make the dish cook faster, plunge them in boiling water for a couple of minutes)
Optional: chopped capsicum, sliced mushrooms, whatever else is in the fridge

Melt the margarine in a heavy-based frying pan. Line the bottom with half the potatoes. Throw in all the vegies, then the grated cheese. Layer the last of the potatoes on the top. Cover with a lid and cook through on a very low heat for about $1/2$ hour. When the potatoes are tender, remove the lid, dot a little margarine on top and brown the whole thing under the grill.

Like every other member of the afternoon program team, I am emphatically not a cook. But I do like to eat. So some years ago I asked various of my friends for their simplest, tastiest recipes. This is one of them.

From Rosemary Greenham, afternoon program producer.

POTATO ROUNDS

1 cup leftover mashed potato
1 egg
1 cup plain flour

Mix all ingredients together. Roll out on a floured board to about ½ cm thickness. Cut into rounds (or use different shaped biscuit cutters). Heat about 1 cm-deep oil in frypan. Fry rounds until light brown, then turn and fry other side. Drain on kitchen paper and spread with apricot jam.

From Edith Thomas of Kallaroo.

DEEP FRIED CAMEMBERT

1 camembert cheese
1 egg
1 tbs milk
Breadcrumbs

Garnish:
Lettuce
Cranberry sauce
Sliced apple

Slice the cheese into 8 segments. Whisk the egg and milk. Coat the cheese with the egg mixture and roll in the breadcrumbs. Refrigerate for 1-2 hours.

Deep fry for 60 seconds, no longer. Garnish with lettuce, sauce and thinly sliced apple and serve immediately.

From Don McRoberts of Attadale.

R.F.T's GARLIC CABBAGE

1 small pot with tight fitting lid
¼ - ½ small cabbage
butter
1 clove garlic

Melt a knob of butter in the saucepan. Add peeled and crushed garlic. Peel off the older, outer leaves of cabbage and cut out the heart. Break up the inner, tightly packed leaves by hand and stuff into saucepan. Do not add water.

Put on very low heat, shaking every now and then to incorporate the butter and garlic with the cabbage. Do not allow to brown. Taste, and serve when still crunchy.

From Ray Twist of Lesmurdie.

Cauliflower is nothing but cabbage with a college education.

Mark Twain, *Pudd'nhead Wilson's Calendar.*

BAKED VEGETABLES TO SERVE WITH A ROAST

Baked vegetables seem to be a favourite with Grapies so we've included a short selection.

CARROTS, PARSNIPS AND SIMILAR-SIZED VEGETABLES
Cut into 10 cm lengths and then halve, lengthwise. Put the halves together and sprinkle with your favourite herbs. Wrap in foil and place in a baking dish with the roast.

ONIONS AND OTHER SOFT VEGETABLES
Peel and wrap in foil parcels. Cook as above. They will cook more quickly than the other vegetables so, if it is a large roast, put them in about 1 hour before carving.

BREAKFAST EGGBAKE

400 gms onions	Salt, pepper
50 gms butter	Pinch nutmeg
350 mls cream	2 tbs chopped parsley
4 eggs	

Slice the onions finely and cook gently in butter until soft. In a bowl, beat together the eggs, cream and milk, adding salt, pepper and nutmeg to taste Add the cooked onions to the mixture and stir in the parsley.

Pour into a baking dish and bake at 140°C for about 1 hour, so that when shaken the centre remains firm. With a large spoon, dollop serves on to the plate.

From Michael Schultz, 720 6WF breakfast program presenter. This recipe is from Geoff Jansz' Taking The Freshest Approach *and is reprinted with kind permission from the publishers.*

JM'S SAVOURY

1 piece of bread
1 pear, thinly sliced
Stilton cheese, thinly sliced
Watercress, chopped
Ground black pepper

Toast the bread and butter. Top with watercress, a couple of pear slices and sliced Stilton. Grill or bake until cheese melts, sprinkle with freshly ground black pepper to taste and devour immediately.

Cheap, quick and wholesome!

From Derek Forster of Inglewood.

BELINDA'S CHEESEY EGG

1 thick slice of bread
approximately 3 rounded tbs grated cheese
1 egg separated

Butter the bread and put onto a baking tray. Place egg yolk in the centre of bread and surround it with $2/3$ of the cheese. Whisk the egg white and fold in the remainder of the cheese. Pile this on top.

Bake in hot oven at 225°C for 10 minutes.

Ideal for a lunch or supper snack, or served with salad makes a quick main course.

From Pat of Roleystone.

CHEESE STICKS

3 sheets puff pastry
1 egg white, beaten
180 gms tasty cheese, grated
1 tbs paprika/curry powder

Cut each pastry sheet into 2 cm strips and brush with beaten egg white. Take two strips of pastry and criss-cross each strip alternately to form one stick.

Place sticks on a greased oven tray and sprinkle with grated cheese.

Sift paprika and curry powder over the top. Bake at 210°C for 7-10 minutes.

From Sonja Siroen of Kelmscott.

IMPOSSIBLE QUICHE

3 eggs, lightly beaten
½ cup self-raising flour, sifted
1 cup milk
60 gms melted butter
1 carrot, grated

1 cup zucchini, grated
Small can sweetcorn, drained
1 onion, chopped
1 cup grated cheese

Heat oven to 180°C. Meanwhile, gently mix all the ingredients together and pour into a greased ovenproof dish. Bake for ½ hour, or until set.

The vegetables can be adapted to suit personal taste. Salmon and tuna can also be substituted, just don't overdo the total quantity.

Sliced tomato and grated cheese can be added on top, for a very appealing dish. Serve with a salad for a satisfying meal.

From Mary Miller of Nedlands.

It is not really an exaggeration to say that peace and happiness begin, geographically, where garlic is used in cooking.

Marcel Boulestin.

VEGETARIAN LASAGNE

1 pkt instant lasagne sheets
1 tin or cup of chopped mushrooms
1 large tin peeled tomatoes
2 tbs tomato paste
6 washed spinach leaves
500 gms ricotta or cottage cheese
Extra grated cheese

Oil
2 garlic cloves
1 onion
Basil, oregano
Parmesan cheese
1 egg

Heat oil, add chopped garlic and onion. Cook lightly, adding tomatoes, tomato paste and herbs. Meanwhile, steam spinach until tender. Mix ricotta cheese and parmesan to taste, beat in egg.

Layer lasagne sheets, all the cheese mixture, spinach, half the tomato sauce and mushrooms. Add the second layer of lasagne sheets and the rest of the sauce. Top with extra grated cheese.

Cook at 180°C for 15-20 minutes.

From Virginia O'Keeffe of Roleystone.

CURRIED CORN FRITTERS WITH MINTED SOUR CREAM

1 cup plain flour
2 tsp curry powder
2 eggs, beaten
1 medium onion, grated
310 gm can corn, drained

Cream:
1 cup sour cream
1 tbs chopped mint
$3/4$ cup milk

Sift flour and curry powder into a large bowl. Make a well in the centre. Stir in eggs and milk. Mix to a smooth batter. Allow to stand for $1/2$ hour. Stir in onion and corn. Divide into small fritters and shallow fry for 2 minutes each side. Drain and serve with minted sour cream.

To make the cream, combine sour cream and mint in a small bowl. Mix ingredients well.

From Beth Giles of Margaret River.

KELLY'S SESAME BURGERS

Total of 2 cups grated beetroot, zucchini, sweet potato, carrot
1 cup sesame seeds
Dash soy sauce
Flour and water to make a stiff dough

Mix vegetables and sesame seeds. Add soya sauce and enough flour and water to make a stiff paste. Shape into patties.

Cook in a heavy based pan in a little oil until brown on one side, turn and cook other side. Press down on patties while cooking to make them stick together.

From Antony Tickle of Balcatta.

There is in every cook's opinion
No savoury dish without an onion:
But lest your kissing should be spoiled
The onion must be thoroughly boiled.

Jonathan Swift.

VEGETARIAN CHILLI CON CARNE

1 onion, finely chopped
1-2 capsicums, roughly chopped
800 gms can tomatoes, roughly chopped — keep juice
740 gms can red kidney beans, mashed well — keep juice
420 gms can corn kernels, strained
4-5 tbs medium taco sauce (half a small jar)
1 tbs olive oil

Fry onions and capsicum in the olive oil until onions are transparent. Add tomatoes and beans, cook for 5 minutes, stirring once. Pour corn kernels on top of the mixture, and pour the taco sauce on the top of that. Cook for 5 minutes at medium/low heat before stirring.

Cook for another 5 minutes without a lid, then place lid on pan and cook, stirring occasionally, for 10-15 minutes.

Serve on a bed of steamed, microwaved or baked vegetables of your choice, along with crusty bread.

For vegetarian nachos, omit the corn and cook the mixture as above. Place 200 gms corn chips on the bottom of a casserole dish, pour desired amount of chilli mixture over the chips and sprinkle with grated cheese. Bake in a moderate oven until cheese melts and browns.

I have found this recipe often fools meat eaters as its texture and spicy flavour disguise the fact that it doesn't contain meat.

From Charlene Crommelin of Hamersley.

SPINACH ROLLS

6-8 leaves fresh silverbeet, washed and chopped
2 eggs
Filo pastry (2 sheets per roll)
200 gms cottage cheese with chives
¼ cup oil
Pepper to taste
Sesame seeds

Place thinly chopped silverbeet, cottage cheese and pepper in a bowl and mix well. Blend 2 eggs with oil and add to mixture. Again, mix well. Place 2 sheets of filo pastry on baking tray.

Place mixture in the middle and roll into a basic 'sausage roll' shape. Oil to join ends. Sprinkle with sesame seeds. Bake 15-20 minutes at 180°C, or until silverbeet is cooked. Test with cake tester. Cool and eat.

Rolls can be as full of mixture as you like. You judge the amount per roll. Great for lunches, snacks or anytime.

From Beth Giles of Margaret River.

ROASTED RED CAPSICUMS

2 large red capsicums
2 large red tomatoes
1 tin anchovy fillets — keep oil
Olive oil
2 cloves garlic
Pepper

Preheat oven to 180°C. Oil a shallow roasting tin. Wash and cut capsicums in half leaving stems intact. Cut through stems, as this helps them to keep their shape. Place in roasting tin.

Plunge tomatoes into boiling water and peel. Cut tomatoes in quarters and place two quarters in capsicum boats. Divide the anchovy fillets in 4 and chop with scissors into boats. Repeat with the garlic.

Dribble anchovy oil over capsicums, along with 1tsp olive oil per capsicum half. Add freshly ground black pepper.

Place in oven on the top shelf for 50 minutes. Serve with fresh bread.

From Ali Nuñez of Shoalwater.

GRILLED POLENTA

This isn't strictly vegetarian as it uses chicken stock. If you like, you can substitute vegetable stock.

185 gms polenta	3 tbs butter
750 mls chicken stock	2 tbs parmesan cheese
Salt, pepper to taste	Olive oil

Boil stock. Add polenta and stir uncovered for 10 minutes. Add butter, cheese, salt and pepper. Spread on oiled oblong trays or baking dish and allow to cool.

Cut into squares, brush both sides with olive oil. Grill or pan fry in oil until golden in colour.

From Gwen of Thornlie.

Beans, beans, the musical fruit
The more you eat the more you toot.
The more you toot, the better you feel.
So eat your beans with every meal.

Thomas Tanssik.

ZUCCHINI SLICE

4 medium zucchinis	1 cup self-raising flour, sifted
1/2 cup carrot	1/4 cup vegetable oil
1 cup cheese	3 eggs
1 onion, chopped	Fresh rosemary, basil,
2 rashers bacon	Parsley
1/2 cup brown rice, cooked	Ground black pepper

Melt a knob of butter in a frypan. Add onion and chopped bacon and fry until soft. Grate zucchini, carrot and cheese, and place in a bowl with the flour. Add bacon and onion and mix well. Place mixture in a prepared baking dish.

Beat eggs, add fresh herbs and pepper to taste. Add oil and whisk thoroughly. Pour into baking dish. Bake at 180°C for 40 minutes.

From Alison of Beckenham.

PARSLEY PESTO

Large bunch parsley
Olive oil
Salt, pepper, garlic to taste

Pine nuts or walnuts
Parmesan cheese

Chop the parsley very finely, either in a food processor or with a mortar and pestle. While stirring with a wooden spoon, gradually add enough olive oil so the mixture is just liquid. Add salt, pepper and garlic. Add crushed nuts.

Grated parmesan cheese can be added now or sprinkled on later.

Use as a sauce for pasta, fish or chicken.

From John Pannell of Falcon.

STUFFED NASTURTIUM LEAVES

Use good-sized, fresh leaves, cut off the stems. Blanch leaves briefly in boiling salted water to make them pliable. The stems can be chopped and added to the filling.

Use the same filling as you would for any Greek or Middle Eastern stuffed vegetable. Put a heaped tablespoon of filling in the middle of a leaf, fold the edges over and roll up like a cigar. You shouldn't have to tie them.

Pack them into a pan with a lid and just cover with water or stock. Cook very gently until the filling is cooked, usually about an hour depending on the filling. Serve cold.

From John Pannell of Falcon.

SWEDISH SPICED RED CABBAGE (SURKÅL)

1 small red cabbage, sliced
60 gms butter
1 apple, sliced
1 tsp caraway seeds

1 tbs sugar
4 tbs cider vinegar
$\frac{1}{2}$ tsp salt (optional)

Remove the white core of the cabbage and wash leaves. In a heavy-based saucepan, melt butter. Add other ingredients. Cook on low heat until cabbage is tender. Stir occasionally with a wooden spoon.

This can be served with practically anything. Swedish people serve it with fish or meat.

From Connie of City Beach.

MEAT & POULTRY

MOTHER-IN-LAW'S EGG & BACON PIE

6-12 eggs
2 sheets of frozen buttered puff pastry

4-5 rashers bacon
Heaps of parsley

Let the pastry sheets defrost. Grease a normal pie dish and bung in one of the sheets. Grill your bacon and chop into chunky bits. Get rid of the rind and fat.

Chop parsley. Toss some of the bacon in the pie, then a handful of parsley. Then break 4-5 eggs into the dish. Avoid breaking the yolks. Then add more bacon, more parsley and more eggs until it all comes to just below the brim of the pie dish. Place the second pastry sheet on top and trim to fit. Any leftover pastry can be used to make a snappy design for the lid. Brush with milk, put some holes in the lid.

Bake at 200°C until golden brown. Turn oven down to 150°C and bake until you sense the eggs are cooked.

Serve hot or cold. For variation, you can add some corn kernels, fried onion, cheese or smoked salmon. Enjoy!

From Ted Bull, 720 6WF evening program presenter.

FIGS AND PROSCIUTTO

12 fresh figs
12 very thin slices prosciutto
24 black olives

Quarter the figs. Place on a large platter with slices of prosciutto and black olives. If possible, the prosciutto should be sliced in the shop on the day you use it as it dries out very quickly.

Serve as appetiser or entree.

From Peter Holland, 720 6WF afternoon program and Grapevine presenter. This recipe is from Ian Parmenter's Consuming Passions *and is reprinted with kind permission of Ian Parmenter and David Evans.*

If you throw a lamb chop in the oven, what's to keep it from getting done?

Joan Crawford in the film *The Women.*

SAUSAGE STEW

500 gms sausages
2 large onions, chopped
250 gms bacon, chopped
1 tin tomato puree
425 gms tin baked beans
Oil
500 gms beef stock

Boil sausages in salted water and simmer for 5 minutes. Drain and rinse under cold water. Leave to cool. Saute onions and bacon in a little oil.

Add tomato puree and simmer. Slice sausages to 1 cm thick, add to pot along with baked beans. Stir in beef stock to desired consistency.

Serve with mashed potato.

I am a food coordinator at a child care centre and this is one of the children's favourites.

From Carolyn Garrod-Raynor of Toodyay.

MEAT LOAF

1 kg minced steak
1 pkt soup mix (mushroom or celery)
½ cup tomato paste or tomato sauce
1½ cups breadcrumbs
2 eggs
¾ cup water

Pre-heat oven to 150°C. Combine all ingredients thoroughly. Bake in a loaf tin for about 1 hour.

This recipe can be varied by adding grated carrot, grated zucchini or finely diced celery. Paprika or curry powder can be added to taste.

Slice to serve, or freeze immediately.

From Kathryn of Duncraig.

CORNED BEEF HASH

340 gms can corned beef
1 large onion, sliced
1 large carrot, sliced thinly
1 cup peas or corn
1 tin tomatoes
1 beef stock cube
Worcestershire sauce
4-5 sliced raw potatoes

Put all ingredients in layers in casserole dish. Pour over the chopped tomatoes with juice combined with stock cube and Worcestershire sauce.

Bake at 200°C for approximately 1 hour, or until most of the liquid has evaporated.

Serve with crusty bread.

From Jacquie Carrick of Connolly.

A LA BULLERS

4 pieces oyster blade steak
1 pkt French Onion soup mix
1 tbs red wine
Small tin mushrooms in butter sauce
Tomatoes, sliced
Green capsicum, sliced
1 tbs Worcestershire sauce

Place all ingredients in casserole dish and bake at 200°C for about 1 hour, or until steak is tender. Serve with mashed potatoes and vegetables.

From Jacquie Carrick of Connolly.

Home from my office to my Lord's lodgings, where my wife got ready a very fine dinner: viz a dish of marrow bones. A leg of mutton. A loin of veal. A dish of fowl, three pullets and two dozen larks. A great tart. A neat's tongue. A dish of anchovies. A dish of prawns; and cheese.

Samuel Pepys.

SAUSAGE CURRY

1 onion	1 tbs flour
750 gms sausages	1 tsp curry powder
1 apple	$1/2$ tsp mustard
2 large tomatoes	1 cup water

Saute onion until tender. Chop sausages and place in casserole dish. Chop apple and tomatoes and put on top of sausages. Place onion in casserole dish.

Mix flour, curry powder and mustard with water, then add to casserole.

Bake at 180°C for approximately 1 hour, stirring twice.

From Julie of Warwick.

FRUITED PORK CHOPS

Pork chops	2 tbs dried apricots
Salt, pepper, celery to taste	2 tbs raisins
$1/3$ cup white wine or sweet sherry	1 tbs brown sugar
Granny Smith apples, unpared and sliced	

Place chops in an oven dish with seasoning. Add wine. Lay apples on top, followed by raisins, sugar and apricots. Cover and cook on a low heat for 45 minutes, or until cooked.

From Jessie Cammack of Gosnells — her own variation of an old recipe .

LAZY TASTY PORK CASSEROLE

1 large pork fillet
1 large brown onion
1 clove garlic
2 medium tomatoes
1 tbs chopped chives
2 chicken stock cubes

Remove excess skin from fillet. Cut diagonally into slices approximately 1 cm thick. Gently beat with a steak hammer until the pieces are approximately 6-8 cm round.

Peel and slice onions into rings. Peel and chop garlic and slice tomatoes. Lightly brown the onions, garlic and meat in a frypan. Dissolve the stock cubes in 2 cups boiling water.

Place half the onions and garlic in the bottom of a shallow casserole dish and cover with a layer of tomatoes. Place the pork on the tomatoes, then cover with the remainder of the tomatoes, onions and garlic. Sprinkle chives over the top and add stock.

Cover casserole dish, place in hot oven until boiling (about 15 minutes). Then turn down heat immediately to 100°C and cook for 1 hour.

Serve with jacket potatoes and broccoli.

Veal may be used instead of pork.

From Iris Ward of Ardross.

VEAL OREGANO

750 gms diced veal
1 small can tomato soup
440 gms can tomatoes
1 egg
Breadcrumbs
1 onion, chopped
2 cloves garlic, crushed
Salt, pepper to taste
1 tsp oregano
$\frac{1}{2}$ green capsicum
2 sticks celery

Dip pieces of veal in egg and coat in breadcrumbs. Fry in hot oil. Remove from heat, brown onions. Return meat to pan with soup and all other ingredients. Cook for 20 minutes, or until meat is tender.

From Marita Jennings of Mount Hawthorn.

CHICKEN SURPRISE

1 boneless chicken breast, skin removed   1 tbs fruit chutney
1 bacon rasher, rind removed

Cook chicken breast and bacon. Wrap bacon around the chicken breast. Heat the fruit chutney and serve on top of the chicken and bacon.

From Elvor Moore of Quinns Rocks.

SALAMUGUNDY

250 gms chopped bacon
6-8 large pieces Italian bread, sliced
6 tomatoes, sliced
Salt, pepper
Chilli powder
200 gms tasty cheese, grated

Select the large, long, narrow slices from a round loaf of Italian bread. Spread with margarine or butter. Cover bread slices with the bacon pieces, then tomato slices and lastly, cheese. Press down until firm. Season with salt, pepper and a little chilli powder.

Bake in a very hot oven until nicely brown and everything is sizzling. Take out and cool before cutting into finger-sized slices.

Someone asked me what they were called, and a man at a party said, 'Call them Salamugundys.' That was 40 years ago!

From E Holly of Kardinya.

5 MINUTE CHILLI BEEF

2 tbs oil (preferably grapeseed)
200 gms fillet or scotch fillet cut into strips
Small onion
1 stick celery, thinly sliced
Other vegetables to taste
1 tbs chilli paste
1 tbs laksa paste
2 tsp ginger
$1/2$ cup tomato sauce
2 tsp soy sauce
$1/4$ cup water

Heat oil in large frypan or wok. When oil is smoking, add sliced onion and celery. Saute rapidly until just soft. Add fillet strips and all other ingredients, ensuring heat is not reduced. Stir thoroughly and fry for 3 minutes.

Variations of this stir-fried beef recipe were sent by several Grapies including Peter Field and Angela Shannon.

FILO PASTRY MEAT AND VEGETABLE PARCELS

500 gms pork or chicken mince
1 carrot
1 parsnip
1 potato
$1/4$ cabbage
1 cup grated cheese
Filo pastry

Small amount pumpkin
1 onion or leek
1 stick celery
1 cup broccoli/cauliflower
1 beaten egg
1 tbs cornflour

Grate all vegetables finely or put in food processor. Mix meat and vegetables together and stir in the cheese. Season to taste. Mix cornflour with a little water and add to mixture. Add beaten egg, mix thoroughly.

Place heaped tablespoons of mixture onto 3 sheets filo pastry and fold into a triangle or large roll. Bake at 180°C for 15-20 minutes. Serve hot or cold.

From Julia Phillips of Cloverdale.

LAMB ROAST WITH REDCURRANT SAUCE

200 mls sour cream
2 crushed garlic cloves
1 tbs wholegrain mustard
Salt, pepper to taste

250 mls red wine
2 tbs redcurrant or
Cranberry jelly
1 leg of lamb

Mix 60 mls of the sour cream with garlic and mustard. Season to taste and spread over the lamb. Place in oven and roast in the usual way.

When cooked, remove lamb from roasting pan and keep warm. Into the pan put the wine, the remaining sour cream and redcurrant jelly. Place on heat and stir until it boils. While carving the lamb, allow the sauce to cook and thicken slightly, stirring now and again. Pour over sliced meat.

From Mrs M Girdlestone of Osborne Park.

*Yet smell roast meat, beheld a huge fire shine,
And cooks in motion with their clean arms bared.*

Byron, *Don Juan, Canto V. St 50.*

SAUSAGE STROGANOFF

2 grilled sausages per person
1 onion, chopped
1 large can cream of mushroom soup
Garlic to taste
$\frac{1}{2}$ can water

Saute onions and garlic in oil until soft. Add sliced sausages, soup and water. Heat through and serve with noodles, pasta or vegetables.

Modified from the recipe which first appeared in The Pennywise Cookbook, *produced by the Milk Marketing Board of England & Wales over 20 years ago.*

From R Buxton of East Victoria Park.

*Nearer as they came, a genial savour
Of certain stews and roast-meats, and pilaus,
Things which in hungry mortal's eyes find favour.*

Byron, *Don Juan, Canto V. St 47.*

BEEF IN PLUM SAUCE

Baby beef steak, sliced very thinly
Vegetables, cut into bite-sized pieces and steamed lightly
Can of spicy plum sauce

Cook the beef in a small amount of oil, until the meat is sealed. Add a generous amount of plum sauce (2-3 tbs), and continue to cook. This should take just 2-3 minutes. Remove steak and vegetables, coat with sauce and serve immediately with rice.

From Jennifer Pitcher of Scarborough.

A MEAL IN A POT

500 gms minced beef
2 brown onions, sliced
2 sticks celery, chopped
½ small cabbage, shredded
½ cup rice
250 gms beans
2 cups water
1 pkt Chicken Noodle Soup
1 dsp curry powder
1 dsp butter/margarine

Brown onions in butter. Add mince and brown. Simmer, then add curry powder, soup rice, celery and water. Cook for 30 minutes. Stir in beans and cabbage. Cook for a further 15 minutes.

From Robin Browne of Rivervale.

CHICKEN IN ORANGE

Juice and rind of 1 large orange
1 tsp tarragon
½ cup sherry
Wheat-hearts
Chicken pieces
Salt, pepper

Mix the juice, rind, tarragon, sherry and seasoning together well. Marinate the chicken pieces for several hours, turning occasionally. Remove from marinade and coat in Wheat-hearts. Put coated chicken in casserole and cover with the marinade.

Bake at 180°C for 1¼ hours. Turn pieces to ensure even cooking.

From Sonia Grant in Yokine.

GREEK CHICKEN

1 young chicken
Cocktail glass of brandy
Same quantity fresh cream
Salt, pepper to taste
Butter
Marjoram
Lemon

Joint the chicken according to size and tenderness. Fry lightly in butter and marjoram until golden brown.

Pour the brandy over the chicken and let it simmer. Pour on the cream and serve immediately.

This can also be made without the cream.

From Sonia Grant of Yokine.

LECSO (pronounced 'Letcho')

5-6 yellow capsicums
1 large onion
3 continental frankfurts
2-3 tbs tomato paste
3 eggs
2 tbs sour cream
Oil, salt to taste
Paprika

Place oil in pan. Add sliced capsicums, onion and frankfurts, along with tomato paste and salt. Saute on a low heat until soft.

Add paprika. Break eggs over mixture and stir in lightly. Cook until set. Add sour cream.

Serve hot or cold with crusty bread.

From Edith Thomas of Kallaroo.

CHICKEN BAKED IN BARBECUE SAUCE

1 skinless chicken piece per person
Sauce:
1 cup lo-cal tomato sauce or tomato puree
1 dsp onion flakes
1 tbs soy sauce
$1/2$ tsp mustard
pinch cayenne pepper
1 clove garlic, crushed

Place all sauce ingredients in a basin and mix together. Place chicken pieces in ovenproof tray, spoon over sauce. Bake for 1 hour or until tender. Serve hot or cold. Serve with salad or vegetables.

Chicken can be replaced with firm white fish steaks or cutlets and cooking time reduced to 30 minutes.

A recipe sent in by an anonymous Grapie.

CHICKEN IN COKE

8 chicken pieces
1 pkt French Onion Soup
1 can Coca Cola

Place chicken pieces in a casserole dish. Sprinkle soup mix on top and pour Coca Cola on top of that. Cover and cook in microwave approximately 30 minutes, or until cooked.

From Lois of Mandurah.

RENOIR CHICKEN

Chicken pieces
Oil, butter
2 onions, finely chopped
2 tomatoes, peeled
Garlic, bay leaf, parsley, thyme, pepper to taste
Chopped mushrooms
Black olives

Brown chicken pieces in oil and butter. Remove from casserole and keep warm. Discard oil and return pieces to the pot with a little more butter. Add onions, tomatoes, garlic, herbs, pepper and a little hot water.

Cover and simmer over a low heat until tender. Stir from time to time. About $\frac{1}{2}$ hour before serving, add mushrooms and olives.

This recipe is attributed to Mme Renoir, and according to an old art magazine was Renoir's favourite dish.

From Pat of Como.

ROAST CHICKEN, ITALIAN STYLE

Chicken pieces
Onions, sliced in rings — enough to give a generous covering to the bottom of a roasting dish
One bulb of garlic — cloves unpeeled
Fresh rosemary
Olive oil

Place onion rings in bottom of roasting pan. Place chicken pieces on top. Sprinkle cloves of garlic around the chicken. Top with stalks of rosemary and drizzle olive oil over the top.

Bake in a moderate/hot oven for 1 hour, or until chicken is cooked.

You can also put potatoes into the pan but they may go a bit soggy.

From Fiona Guthrie, Drive program presenter on 720 6WF.

COLD CURRY SAUCE FOR CHICKEN

2 tbs oil
2 onions, finely chopped
1 rounded tbs curry powder
1 tbs apricot jam
1 tbs mango chutney
$1/2$ cup tomato sauce
$1/2$ cup low-fat mayonnaise
$1/2$ cup lightly whipped cream

Heat oil and fry onions until soft. Add curry powder and cook for 1 minute, stirring a few times. Add chutney, jam and tomato sauce. Mix well, then cool.

Gently fold in mayonnaise and cream. Cool before serving.

From Sue Wilson of Duncraig.

SIMPLE SIMON CHICKEN

1 chicken piece per person
1 pkt savoury cheese biscuits, finely crushed
$1/2$ cup salad oil
2 tsp salt (optional)

Add salt to biscuits and mix. Pour salad oil onto a second plate. Dip chicken pieces into salad oil, or brush on. Then coat well with biscuit crumbs.

Place on a large, ungreased ovenware plate. Bake at 180°C for about 1 hour, until golden brown and tender. Do not turn while cooking.

Serve hot or cold.

From Kaye Greening of Jandakot.

ASPARAGUS CHICKEN CASSEROLE

1 kg chicken pieces, skin removed
340 gms can asparagus pieces, drained
1 cup cream, yoghurt or sour cream
440 gm can Cream of Asparagus soup, undiluted
1 cup grated tasty cheese
Black pepper, salt to taste

Put chicken pieces in casserole dish. Combine all over ingredients and cover chicken. Season to your taste with salt or ground black pepper.

Bake at 180°C for $1-1\frac{1}{2}$ hours or microwave on High for 30-40 minutes.

From Catherine Wyllie of Joondanna.

SPEEDY CHICKEN MUSHROOM FILLETS

4-6 chicken fillets
Seasoned flour
1 tbs oil
1 can sliced mushrooms in butter sauce
1 tbs butter/margarine
Small glass brandy
$1/_3$ cup cream
Salt, pepper to taste

Coat chicken with flour and cook in oil and butter until golden brown and tender. Remove and keep warm. Drain oil from pan and add mushrooms, brandy and cream. Bring to the boil and season with salt and pepper. Simmer gently for 3 minutes.

Spoon sauce over chicken and serve immediately.

From Phyl of Mundijong.

GREEN CASSEROLE CHICKEN

1 onion
1 tsp garlic
90 gms butter
300 gms tin mushrooms in butter sauce
$1/_2$ cup tomato sauce
1 cup frozen green beans
1 cup frozen peas
1 tbs sugar
Salt, pepper
Chilli powder to taste
1 tbs Worcestershire sauce
1 kg chicken pieces

Saute onions and garlic in butter. Put all ingredients except chicken in a casserole dish and microwave on High for 3 minutes. Add chicken and microwave on High for 35 minutes. Serve with baked potatoes.

From Sue Goddard of Gosnells.

FISH & SEAFOOD

POP'S CURRIED PRAWNS

300 gms prawn meat
1 dsp butter or margarine
1 tbs curry powder, to taste
Sugar, salt, pepper

600 mls milk
1 tbs cornflour
1 onion, chopped

Fry onions in butter until soft, not brown. Add curry powder and stir for 1 minute. Add milk and heat. Thicken with cornflour softened in some milk or water. When thick, add prawns and season to taste with sugar, salt and pepper.

Simmer for a couple of minutes and serve with plain steamed rice.

From Merle Baxter of Lesmurdie.

SLOSHED SQUID

Couple of handfuls of fresh squid
2 tbs tomato paste
Salt
Cayenne pepper

Black Bean sauce
Soy sauce
½ cup vinegar

Remove squid heads and tentacles by sticking index finger down each tube and scooping out the innards (they're quite clean to handle). Slice the squid into rings and throw them into a saucepan.

Add tomato paste, salt to taste and a slosh of black bean and soy sauce. Add vinegar and a shake or 6 of cayenne pepper. Cover with water and cook.

Every 5 minutes or so, try a piece of squid to see if it's tender. Once done, if there's any left, put it in a jar along with the sauce and top with olive oil. Leave in the refrigerator for a couple of days.

Sloshed squid makes a beaut base for a common person's seafood cocktail. Just add fresh crab meat, prawns and/or mussels on top.

From Lee Evans of Palmyra.

FISH MORNAY

Fresh breadcrumbs
2 tbs parmesan cheese
2 tbs butter/margarine
$1/2$ cauliflower
$1/2$ broccoli
1 carrot

60 gms canola margarine
$1/3$ cup plain flour
500-750 mls milk
$1/2$ cup grated cheese
720 gms white fish fillets
1 corn cob

Mix breadcrumbs, parmesan and chopped butter together and reserve. Chop vegetables into bite-sized pieces, remove kernels from cob and steam all vegetables until firm but tender.

Make cheese sauce in the usual way using flour, margarine, milk and cheese.

Break fish fillets into bite-sized pieces and add to cheese sauce.

Place vegetables on the bottom of a greased lasagne dish. Pour sauce over the top and cover with breadcrumb mixture. Bake at 180°C for 20 minutes or until golden brown.

From Rita Robertson of Quindalup.

FILET DE GUMMY SHARK AUX HERBES

1 Gummy Shark fillet per person
Mixed herbs
Lemon juice
Butter/margarine

Soak the fillets in water for 2 minutes. A good fillet should not go flaky and fall apart. Make sure there are no bones left in the fish.

Take some foil and put it into squares large enough to wrap each fillet. Put a dab of butter on each piece of foil then place the fish on the dab.

Squeeze lemon juice on the fish and sprinkle herbs over the top. Wrap foil as if it were somebody's birthday present, and put the packages in the oven.

Bake at 150°C for $1/4$ hour.

From Peter of Maylands.

> *Fish should swim thrice: first it should swim in the sea ... then it should swim in butter, and at last, sirrah, it should swim in good claret.*
>
> Jonathan Swift, *Polite Conversation.*

FISH MINESTRONE

2 litres fish stock
440 gms tin tomatoes
3-4 carrots, peeled & diced
2-3 large potatoes, peeled & diced
3-4 pieces celery, chopped
2 onions, finely chopped
3-4 cloves garlic, crushed
1 dsp grated ginger
2 tbs dry tarragon
2 tbs olive oil
$1/4$ cup small elbow pasta
1 zucchini, diced

Place oil in heavy-based stockpot. Saute garlic, onion and tarragon until soft. Add stock, tomatoes and chopped vegetables. Bring to the boil and simmer until vegetables are cooked. Bring back to the boil, add pasta. Cook for 10 minutes, stirring. Reduce heat and simmer for 20 minutes or until pasta is ready. Add pepper to taste and serve with croutons. Sprinkle parmesan cheese on top.

From Rita Robertson of Quindalup.

A QUICK SCALLOP RECIPE

1 bread roll
1 tsp butter
Handful of scallops

2 bacon rashers
Pepper, salt

Remove the top half of the bread roll. Butter inside and fill with scallops. Season with pepper and salt and cover with bacon. Place the roll lid on and bake at 180°C for 25 minutes.

From Jenny McDonald of Doubleview.

TASTY BAKED FISH

4 fish fillets
1 cup of your favourite cheese, grated
$1/4$ cup each of cream, milk and sherry

Salt, pepper

Grease a shallow dish. Pop in the fish, top with seasoning and cheese. Combine cream, milk and sherry, then add to fish.

Bake at 180°C for 20-25 minutes.

Several Grapies sent a version of this recipe, including Irene of Booragoon and Karen of Bayswater.

CRAB QUICHE

1 flan case
125 gms crab meat
1 tbs spring onions, finely chopped
1 tbs parsley, finely chopped
1 tbs chives, chopped
4 tbs whole kernel corn

$1/2$ tsp chilli powder
Pepper, salt, nutmeg
$1/2$ cup cream
$1/2$ cup milk
1 tbs dry sherry
2 eggs, beaten

Combine all ingredients and pour into flan case. Bake at 200°C for 10 minutes. Reduce heat to 180°C and bake for a further 15 minutes, or until quiche is set and golden. Serve warm.

From John and Ghonda Mackin of Mandurah.

CRUNCHY TUNA ROLLS

Slices of bread with crusts removed
425 gm tin tuna
1 onion, finely chopped
2 tbs mayonnaise
$1/2$ cup sour cream
1 cup grated cheese
Chopped parsley

Roll out bread slices with a rolling pin. Mix onion, mayonnaise and sour cream into drained tuna. Combine well and spread onto bread. Roll up and pack rolls into well-greased casserole dish. Sprinkle with grated cheese.

Bake in a hot oven until golden and crunchy.

From Gem of Daglish.

He was a vary valiant man who first adventured on eating of oyster.

Thomas Fuller, *The History of the Worthies of England.*

SMOKED MACKEREL PATÉ

250 gms smoked mackerel
250 gms cream cheese
1 tbs lemon juice
Milk, sour cream or yoghurt to adjust consistency
$1/2$ tbs tomato ketchup
Tabasco to taste
Ground pepper to taste

Defrost mackerel if frozen, remove skin and any bones. Let ingredients reach room temperature before putting in the blender. Blend until smooth and adjust colour with some tomato ketchup, and adjust consistency with milk, sour cream or yoghurt. Remember though, go for a dip not a drip!

Tomato paste can be used, but tomato ketchup gives it a slightly sweeter flavour.

From Mike Webb of South Perth.

TUNA CASSEROLE

1 large can tuna in brine, drained
500 gms pkt spiral noodles
1 can Cream of Chicken, Cream of Mushroom or Vegetable soup
Grated cheese

Cook noodles according to directions. In a casserole dish, combine soup and tuna. Add drained noodles and mix well. Top with grated cheese if desired.

Bake at 180°C for 45 minutes.

Variations of this quick and easy casserole were sent by several Grapies including Lori of Wanneroo and Betty of Fremantle.

FISH PATTIES

1 large can tuna
2-3 cups breadcrumbs
1 egg
Salt, pepper, herbs, chilli to taste
Olive or canola oil

Mix all ingredients except oil in a bowl. Combine well so that mixture is of firm consistency. Shape into patties and shallow fry on each side until golden brown.

Many Grapies sent their version of this popular recipe, including Warren of Glendalough, Sue of Mount Lawley and Alice of Greenwood.

MOCK SCHNAPPER

While not a bona fide fish dish, we felt it deserved a place in this section!

3 large potatoes
1 heaped tbs flour
1 egg
Salt to taste

Grate potatoes. Squeeze out surplus juice. Mix egg and flour into a thick paste. Mix in potatoes and stir.

Using an electric frypan, drop a dessertspoon of mixture into hot oil and cook until brown on bottom. Turn to cook other side. Repeat until all mixture is cooked.

From Ted Dubberlin of Dianella.

But now through friendly seas they softly run,
Painted the mid-sea blue or the shore-sea green,
Still patterned with the vine and grapes in gold.

James Elroy Flecker

LEE'S TUNA AND TOMATO DIP

185 gm can tuna	4 tbs tomato paste
1 block Philadelphia light cream cheese	1 tbs lemon juice
3-5 tbs sweet chilli sauce (to taste)	2 spring onions
Salt, pepper	

Mix all ingredients together in a small bowl. Place in a serving dish and serve with carrot, celery sticks, corn chips or crusty bread. It can also be used as a sandwich spread.

From Leanne Bengough of Floreat.

PASTA & RICE DISHES

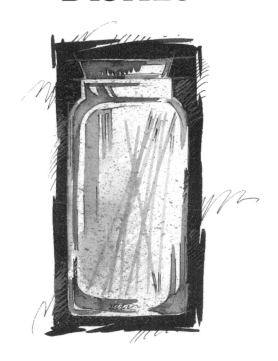

PASTA ALL'AMATRICIANA

1 tbs olive oil
1 onion, chopped
2 cloves garlic
4-6 rashers bacon, chopped

$1/_2$ kg tomatoes, chopped
Basil
500 gms pasta

Cook pasta in lots of water. Heat olive oil. Add bacon and onion and cook gently. When onion is soft, add basil and crushed garlic. Cook 2 minutes.

Add tomatoes and simmer. When pasta is cooked, normally about 10 minutes, drain. Add sauce to pasta and serve with a salad.

This is a great meal for when you are in a hurry. Once everything is chopped, the sauce is ready in 10 minutes. It's quicker than ordering a pizza and much more yummy!

From Jackie Tuffin of Mount Pleasant.

GNOCCHI WITH GORGONZOLA SAUCE

500 gms gnocchi
125 gms Gorgonzola or other blue cheese
250 gms butter
4 tbs cream

Combine butter, cheese and cream in a saucepan. Stir continuously over a low heat. Cook gnocchi and drain. Combine gnocchi and sauce and serve immediately.

Very rich and very delicious, and best followed by a green salad!

From Linda of the Flatlanders Permaculture Group in Beckenham.

EASY TOMATO SAUCE FOR PASTA OR PIZZA

6 ripe tomatoes, roughly chopped
$1/2$ cup wine or water
$1/2$ chopped onion
3 tbs tomato paste
1 clove garlic
2 tbs fresh chopped parsley

Place all ingredients in a dish and microwave on High for 5 minutes. Or cook in a saucepan for 15 minutes.

From Linda Walls of Ballajura.

MUM'S CHICKEN SPAGHETTI

500 gms chicken, skinned and diced
1 onion, chopped
3 very ripe tomatoes
A few pieces of celery
$1/2$ tsp mixed spice
$1/2$ tsp mixed herbs
Salt, pepper
$1/2$-1 cup grated cheese

Brown the onion in oil. Add chicken and brown a little, then add tomatoes, celery, herbs, spices, salt and pepper. Cover and simmer until chicken is cooked.

Cook spaghetti, drain and sprinkle cheese over the top. Mix through once cheese has melted. Add sauce and serve with fresh crusty bread and a green salad.

The leftovers are great cold, in sandwiches, reheated or toasted. The sauce freezes well.

From Jennifer Pitcher of Scarborough.

ATLANTIC COLLEGE SPAGHETTI

1 pkt spaghetti
Olive oil
2 cloves garlic
Handful fresh basil and rosemary
1 onion, chopped
1 sachet tomato paste
3 tbs parmesan
2 tbs tasty cheese
Dash cream

Heat oil and saute onion and garlic until soft. Add herbs and tomato paste, mix well. Remove from heat and add cheese. Mix well, return to very low heat and stir until cheese has melted. Add a dash of cream to make the consistency you require.

Cook spaghetti. Drain, toss in a little butter and serve with sauce, extra parmesan, good friends and robust red wine.

From Sharron of Inglewood.

SPINACH PASTA

1 onion, chopped
4-6 sliced soft tomatoes or 1 can
$1/2$ bunch spinach or silverbeet, well washed, drained and chopped
$1/2$ red capsicum, sliced
2-3 cloves garlic, crushed

Fry onion and garlic in a little oil until tender. Add capsicum and cook for 2 minutes. Add tomatoes and cook 2 minutes. Lastly, add spinach and simmer for a few minutes.

Serve over hot pasta. Add pieces of fetta cheese and a few black olives just before serving.

From Vicky of Kardinya.

BASIL PASTA

2 cups fresh basil leaves
$1/2$ cup olive oil
$1/2$ cup parmesan cheese
$1/4$ cup pine nuts
6 cloves garlic
Salt, pepper, sugar

Wash and dry basil leaves. Puree or blend all other ingredients together. Add a little extra olive oil to make a smooth paste. Pour over cooked pasta and stir through.

From Gwen of Thornlie.

FETTUCINE WITH ASPARAGUS AND SMOKED SALMON

1½ cups chicken stock
8 spring onions, chopped
500 gms fresh egg fettucine, cooked & drained
20 fresh asparagus spears — tips cut off & reserved
200 gms sliced smoked salmon (budget tip: use tuna or red salmon)
30 gms olive oil or butter
300 mls cream

Cook asparagus tips until tender, but still crisp. Refresh in cold water. Reserve. Cook asparagus stalks in stock until tender. Fry spring onions until soft. Blend cream, onions and asparagus stalks until smooth. Combine with salmon strips and toss through fettucine.

From Rosemary Morrow of Booragoon.

The angels in Paradise eat nothing but vermicelli al pomidoro.

Duke of Bovino.

CAROLYN'S HEALTHY CREAMY PASTA SAUCE

3-4 rashers bacon
300 gms fresh mushrooms, sliced
¾ cup ricotta cheese
¾ cup natural yoghurt
1 tbs flour
375g fresh filled pasta or
300 gms dried pasta
4-5 broccoli florets

Cook pasta according to directions. Add broccoli just before pasta is cooked, to blanch.

In a non-stick pan, fry bacon without additional oil, for about 1 minute. Add sliced mushrooms and cook until well done. Combine ricotta cheese, yoghurt and flour. Add to bacon and mushroom mixture and heat through.

Add cooked pasta and broccoli and serve immediately, sprinkled with a little Parmesan cheese.

My kids love this, and it's much healthier than the original version with all that cream.

From Carolyn of Dianella.

PAT'S VERY OWN PASTA HOTCH-POTCH

Cooked mince, drained
Mixed diced vegetables, assorted kinds
1 can 3-Bean Mix, drained
1 can tomatoes
Tomato paste
Paprika
Worcestershire sauce
Herb pepper
Chutney
Herb pepper

Add everything to the vegetables during cooking, and mix gently. Thicken with cornflour or pour off excess liquid for stock. It'll cook in the same amount of time it'll take to cook your favourite pasta.

From Pat MacKenzie of Doubleview.

PASTA Y.E.S.
(Yummiest, Easiest Spaghetti)

300 gms spaghetti
150 gms prosciutto or pancetta, diced
200 gms rocket or English spinach
Black pepper, grated Parmesan cheese
50 mls extra virgin olive oil
Boiling salted water
30 gms pine nuts

Select your wok. A frypan will do, but it'll need to be biggish to fit everything in.

In the wok, dry roast the pine nuts until golden, then get them out in a hurry before you overdo them. Put to one side.

Add pasta to the boiling water. To the empty wok over low heat, add rocket. Cook briefly, stirring. Add the pancetta and stir until rocket is starting to wilt. Add pine nuts.

The pasta should be cooked by now. Drain and add to the wok with oil. Toss and swirl briefly until pasta is coated with oil and meat and greens are evenly distributed. Serve with grated parmesan and pepper.

This looks simple, but tastes brilliant.

From Marshall Martin, 720 6WF music director and Saturday breakfast presenter.

MOZZARELLA NAPOLITANA

50 gms butter
1 chopped onion
1 can tomatoes
150 gms mozzarella cheese, diced
1 tsp sugar

3 tbs parmesan cheese
Black olives
Fresh basil, chopped
1 pkt pasta, cooked

Saute onion in large pan. Add tomatoes, season and stir. Add mozzarella and parmesan. Heat sauce until it bubbles, then add sugar, olives and chopped basil.

Pour sauce over pasta and sprinkle with extra parmesan. Bake at 180°C for 10 minutes.

From Patricia Young of Innaloo.

Rice is born in water and must die in wine.
Old Italian proverb.

PEAK HILL PASTA SAUCE

1 dsp soy sauce
1 dsp Worcestershire sauce
1 tsp mixed herbs
1 tsp granulated garlic
1 beef stock cube

300 gms good beef mince
1 onion, chopped
1 carrot, grated
$\frac{1}{2}$ cup warm water
Tomato sauce

Blend all ingredients except stock cube and tomato paste, and put on lowest heat. Stir frequently to break up any lumps. When onions are cooked and plenty of liquid is present, crumble in the stock cube. Cook for a further 15 minutes then taste.

When satisfied, add a few dollops of good tomato sauce, or a little Tomato Magic (too much tomato will make it acid). Mix well then taste again. When happy with the taste, stir in some fresh, chopped parsley or parsley flakes.

From Ray Twist of Lesmurdie.

ALMOST INSTANT TUNA LASAGNE

185 gm tin tuna, drained and flaked ½ pkt instant lasagne sheets
500 mls cheese sauce or 2 sachets of packet sauce mix
Extra grated cheese

Add the tuna to the cheese sauce. Layer the lasagne sheets with the sauce, starting and finishing with sauce. Top with extra cheese. Bake at 180°C for 40 minutes, until brown on top and lasagne sheets have softened.

It can be frozen after cooking.

From Mary Masters of Padbury.

SPINACH RICE

2 tbs olive oil
1 onion, finely chopped
1 clove garlic, chopped
2 chicken stock cubes
1 cup white rice

2 cups water
1 bunch English spinach
1 tsp cinnamon
Salt, pepper

Fry onion and garlic until brown. Add rest of ingredients. Keep stirring until the mixture bubbles. Simmer for 5 minutes then switch off heat and cover with a clean cloth. An hour later, the rice will be ready, having absorbed all the liquid. It should be fluffy when stirred.

A taste of Cypriot cuisine from Theo Zavros of Kallaroo.

SAVOURY RICE CASSEROLE

1 onion, chopped
500 gms mince meat
1 cup rice
1 pkt Chicken Noodle soup

1 tsp curry powder
250 gms green beans
¼ cabbage, diced
4 cups hot water

Brown the onion and mince in a large saucepan. Add other ingredients, bring to the boil and simmer 15 minutes or until moisture is absorbed.

From Brigitte of Banjup.

SPINACH LASAGNE

1 pkt instant lasagne sheets
1 bunch spinach
1 tbs olive or canola oil
1 onion, finely chopped
2 cups white sauce

3 cloves garlic, crushed
4-5 tomatoes, sliced
2 cups grated cheese
Some chopped chicken

Wash spinach leaves and discard stems. Cook on low heat in a little water until wilted. Drain, cool and chop. Add onion, garlic and chicken. Mix well.

Oil lasagne dish and line with lasagne sheets. Top with half the spinach mixture, cover with tomato slices, then 1 cup of cheese and 1 cup of white sauce.

Repeat. Cover with foil and bake at 180°C for 40 mins. Remove foil and bake for 10 minutes, or until golden brown.

From Rita Robertson of Quindalup.

With a handful of rice and a little dried fish I can make a dozen dishes.

T S Eliot.

TOMATO RISOTTO

3 tbs olive oil
2 onions, chopped
125 gms ham, chopped
2 cups quick cooking brown rice
1 can tomatoes, undrained

3 tbs tomato paste
1 litre chicken stock
1 tbs butter
125 gms parmesan cheese
2 tbs fresh basil

Fry onions and ham in oil until golden. Add rice and cook for a few minutes. Add tomatoes, tomato paste and stock, then cook, stirring frequently until liquid is absorbed and rice is cooked. Stir in the butter, parmesan and basil. Season with pepper. Spoon into a greased ovenproof bowl and bake at 200°C for 10-15 minutes.

From Kate Parker of Coogee.

MEXICAN RICE

500 gms beef mince
5 tbs rice
1 onion, chopped

1 dsp curry powder
425 gm tin tomato soup

Cook rice and onion in a little oil for 3 minutes. Add mince and brown. Mix in tomato soup and same amount of water. Stir well and simmer until liquid is taken up — approximately 45 minutes.

From J Clifford of High Wycombe.

DESSERTS

SLIGO PUDDING

3 large apples, peeled and cored (Granny Smiths are best)
Brown sugar
Lemon juice

For batter:
90 gms margarine or butter
3 tbs milk
1 tbs custard powder
2 tbs sugar
3 tbs self-raising flour

Slice apples and place in greased pie dish. Sprinkle with brown sugar or lemon juice. Cream butter and sugar, add milk, flour and custard powder. Beat well and pour over apples in dish. Bake about 20 minutes in a moderate oven (180°C).

It can be divided and cooked in individual dishes if desired. Adding extra brown sugar and lemon juice makes for a sharpish, treacle-like taste.

From Jean Goadby of Manning. It was one of her mother's recipes and Jean thinks the name comes from Sligo on the north-west coast of the Republic of Ireland.

QUICK PEACH DESSERT

1 can of peach halves Apricot jam
Flaked almonds

Fill well-drained peach halves with a little apricot jam. Sprinkle with toasted flaked almonds. Warm in a moderate (180°C) oven for 5-10 minutes. Serve with whipped cream, ice-cream or both.

Easy, quick and delicious. Leonie tried this and gave it 10 out of 10.

From Patricia Young of Innaloo.

GRANNY'S FUDGE

2 kgs soft brown sugar 500 gms butter
1 tin sweetened condensed milk

Melt the butter and sugar in a heavy saucepan and then add the condensed milk. Bring to the boil and stir. Remove from heat and beat with a wooden spoon until the fudge thickens. Pour into a large greased baking tin and cut into squares just before it gets cold.

From Sonia Grant of Yokine.

PINEAPPLE TIDBITS

30 gms copha Wooden tooth picks
90 gms dark cooking chocolate 425 gm can pineapple pieces

Drain the pineapple well. Pierce each pineapple piece with a toothpick and freeze.

Melt copha and broken chocolate. Dip each frozen pineapple piece into the chocolate mixture and leave to stand on a tray covered with waxed paper. When firm, remove from paper and store in a covered container in the fridge.

From Christine Chantler of Bindoon.

I am not hungry, but thank goodness I am greedy.

Punch, *19th Century.*

RUM PLUMS

1 can dark plums in syrup 2 tbs rum
1 piece of cinnamon stick (about 2 cm)

Drain plums, place in a serving bowl and reserve syrup. Place syrup in a saucepan with cinnamon stick and rum. Simmer for 10 minutes until 'more syrupy'. Remove from heat and strain over plums. Cover and refrigerate until well chilled.

Delicious served topped with fresh cream, ice-cream or natural yoghurt.

Ideal for the 'do ahead' dinner party dessert.

From Jean Caley of Samson.

MANGO MOUSSE

1 carton whipping cream 1 can mangoes
1 pkt lemon jelly

Drain the mangoes, heat juice and dissolve the jelly in it. Cool the mixture. Whip the cream, add the jelly and the chopped mangoes. Chill and serve.

From Anne Hood of Kalamunda.

FRUIT SALAD DESSERT

1 large tin tropical fruit salad 1 pkt small marshmallows
1 kg tub fruit yoghurt (Fruit-of-the-Forest works best)
600 gms cream, beaten until thick

Mix all the ingredients together and refrigerate until ready to serve.

From Eileen Harshaw of Balcatta.

MRS McKINNON'S PASSIONFRUIT JELLY

1 packet of lemon jelly crystals
1 cup boiling water
1 cup milk
1 tbs sugar
1 egg
2 passionfruit

Make jelly with boiling water. Stand until cold, but not set. Beat milk, egg and sugar together. Add to jelly with pulp from the passionfruit. Allow to set.

Serve in individual bowls or large bowl.

From Jean Trawinski of Calista. This recipe was handed down to her by her mother.

PINEAPPLE MARSHMALLOW DESSERT

1 pkt marshmallows, cut into pieces
400 gm can pineapple, very well drained
1 carton cream, thickened well

Mix all ingredients together and refrigerate.

From Betty Riley of South Lake.

PANCAKES FOR PETER'S SWEET TOOTH

1 batch pancake mixture
Walnuts
Egg whites reserved from pancake mixture
Apricot jam
Sugar

Cook pancakes. As each pancake is cooked, spread it with apricot jam and a few chopped walnuts. Continue this until all pancakes are piled above each other on an ovenproof plate.

Make meringue from egg whites and a little sugar. Completely cover the pancake stack and brown in a warm oven.

Best served at once!

From Margaret Gunter of Dunsborough.

PINEAPPLE SURPRISE

1 pkt Butternut Snap biscuits
2 cans crushed pineapple
600 mls cream

Whip the cream and strain the pineapple. Layer in a clear glass bowl as follows: cream, biscuits, pineapple, cream. Decorate with a pineapple ring and cherry in the middle, and mint leaves. Or sprinkle with nuts. Chill in the fridge at least 4 hours or overnight.

From Phyl Fernihough.

RASPBERRY/LOGANBERRY MUSH
(It's very mushy)

$1/2$ sponge cake
3 or 4 tins fruit (raspberry and/or loganberry)
Sherry to taste
Whipping cream

Break up the cake in the base of a large dish. Soak in sherry. Tip in the drained fruit. Add some of the juice. Cover with whipped cream.

From Anne Todd of Darlington.

FRUIT JELLY

1 pkt pineapple or lemon jelly
1 cup boiling water
1 small tin fruit salad or crushed pineapple
1 egg
$1/2$ cup sugar
1 cup milk

Dissolve jelly in boiling water. Beat egg and sugar, add milk. Beat well. Add to jelly. Add fruit salad or pineapple. Allow to set.

From L Garnett of Myaree. This recipe was taken from Family Favourites, *published by Collie Apex Kindergarten, 1967.*

Custard, n. A detestable substance produced by a malevolent conspiracy of the hen, the cow and the cook.

Ambrose Bierce,
The Enlarged Devil's Dictionary.

RUSSIAN CREAM

600 mls milk
3 dsp caster sugar
2 dsp gelatine, dissolved in cold water
2 eggs
1 tsp almond essence

Mix all ingredients except eggs and heat in saucepan until mixture starts to rise. Take off heat and allow to cool. Separate the eggs, add yolks to mixture when cool. Whisk egg whites and gently stir into mixture with a fork. Pour into dish and leave to set.

From John of Mandurah.

JENNIFER'S APRICOT DELIGHT

1 tin apricot nectar
1 carton whipping cream
2 egg whites
1 tbs gelatine
$1/4$ cup cold water

Put gelatine in cold water and heat in half the apricot nectar until dissolved. Chill until it starts to set. Whip egg whites, whip cream, then mix everything together well.

Place in a serving bowl or smaller individual bowls and chill until set.

From Jennifer McDonald of Doubleview.

GOLDEN PUFFS

Puffs:
1 cup self-raising flour
1 tbs butter
Pinch salt (optional)
1 egg
Milk to mix

Syrup:
1 tbs butter
2 tbs sugar
1 tbs honey
1 tbs golden syrup
1 large cup water

Puffs:
Sift flour and salt. Rub in butter. Add well-beaten egg and enough milk to make a stiff dough. Roll into small balls and drop into boiling syrup.

Syrup:
Put all ingredients in saucepan. Boil slowly for 20 minutes. Keep the lid on the saucepan.

From Jo Polglaze of Doubleview.

QUEEN OF PUDDINGS

2 tbs jam	2 cups milk
1 cup fresh breadcrumbs (soft)	90 gms caster sugar
2 eggs	3 tbs diced fruit

Spread half the jam in an ovenproof dish, placing breadcrumbs on top. Separate the eggs. Combine beaten yolks, milk and 2 tbs sugar over low heat until custard thickens. Pour the custard into the dish. Bake at 150°C for 45 minutes, or until firm.

When slightly cool, spread with remaining jam and top with 2 tbs of the fruit. Beat egg whites until stiff and fold in remaining sugar. Pile onto the custard and top with the remaining fruit. Bake at 180°C for 15 minutes and serve hot.

From Lorraine Randall of Medina. This recipe was originally from the Golden Wattle Cookery Book *and is reprinted with kind permission from the publisher.*

I will make an end of my dinner; there's pippins and cheese to come.

William Shakespear,
Merry Wives of Windsor.

TREACLE PUDDING

125 gms butter	125 gms self-raising flour
125 gms sugar	Lots of golden syrup
2 eggs	

Cream butter and sugar until light and fluffy. Beat eggs, fold into cream mixture gradually. Sieve flour and fold in slowly, beating well. Grease a medium-sized pudding bowl or casserole dish. Pour golden syrup into bottom of bowl. Spread pudding mixture over the top. Bake at 180°C for 30 minutes, or until golden. Serve hot with custard.

From Sharron of Inglewood.

EGGLESS PLUM PUDDING

1 cup plain flour
½ cup sugar
½ tsp nutmeg
pinch salt
½ cup sultanas
½ cup currants
1 tsp mixed peel
1 tbs butter
1 tsp bicarbonate. soda
½ cup boiling water

Place flour, sugar, nutmeg, salt, fruit and mixed peel in a bowl and mix together. Place butter on the top. Dissolve soda in water and pour over other ingredients. Mix well and put in centre of prepared pudding cloth. (Take care not to scald yourself.)

To prepare cloth, dip a pudding cloth in a large pot of boiling water, hold opposite corners, twist and wring out. Spread out cloth and sprinkle with flour.

Tie up pudding in cloth securely. Place in pot and boil for 1¼ hours.

Do not let the water go off the boil.

Serve with white sauce flavoured with cinnamon.

From Trixie of Mandurah.

SHOW ME PUDDING

Batter:
¼ cup butter
2 egg yolks
½ cup flour
½ tsp vanilla essence
fruit, chopped (try peaches, bananas, apples)
¼ cup sugar
3 tbs milk
½ tsp baking powder
pinch salt

Meringue:
2 egg whites
¼ cup sugar

Mix all the batter ingredients together. Spread in 20 cm square pan. Add layers of fruit. To make the meringue, beat together the egg whites and sugar until stiff. Spread meringue mixture on top of fruit.

Bake at 190°C for 20-25 minutes.

From Jessie Cammack of Gosnells.

ALISON'S GOLDEN SYRUP PUDDING

2 cups dates
1 cup self-raising flour
1 tbs margarine
$3/4$ cup milk
1 tbs sugar

Sauce:
1 cup boiling water
$1/2$ cup golden syrup
1 tbs margarine

In an ovenproof dish, sift flour and then rub in margarine until crumbly in texture. Add remaining ingredients and mix until sticky. Pat down so that it is sitting flat in the dish. Mix the sauce ingredients together in a jug and pour over the mixture. Bake at 180°C for 30-40 minutes.

If you use non-fat milk it is a very low-fat recipe. My friend Alison is a dietitian and recommends this as a tasty, sweet, low-fat dessert.

From Sally Gatt-Lodding of Victoria Park.

CAKES, BISCUITS, BREAD

ANZAC BISCUITS

125 gms butter
2 tbs golden syrup
$1/2$ tsp baking soda
2 tbs boiling water

1 cup rolled oats
1 cup plain flour
$3/4$ cup coconut
1 cup sugar

Combine the butter and the golden syrup in a small bowl. Microwave for 2 minutes on High. Preheat oven to 180°C. Mix the soda with the boiling water. Add to melted butter mixture. Combine all the dry ingredients and mix into the butter. Place teaspoons of mixture on a lightly greased pizza tray. Place on a low rack and bake for 15 minutes.

Makes approximately 30.

From Maxine O'Donnell of Armadale. This recipe was originally from Sharp's The Complete Microwave Cookbook *and is reprinted with kind permission from the publisher.*

> *The only way to get rid of temptation is to yield to it.*
>
> Oscar Wilde.

GRANDMA'S CHEESE MUFFINS

1 cup self-raising flour
1 cup milk
1 cup grated cheese

Mix the ingredients together and spoon into greased muffin tins. Sprinkle some parmesan cheese on top and bake in a hot oven for 10 minutes.

From Leanne Rogerson of Jolimont. Given to her by her grandmother, Mrs Edna Cheffins, who also listens to the Grapevine.

LEMONADE SCONES

4 cups flour
small carton of cream
pinch salt
$3/4$ can of lemonade

Mix all ingredients together and knead. Cut into scones and place on a greased tray. Cook at 220°C for 10-12 minutes.

From Mary Mell of Stratton.

BEER BREAD

3 cups self-raising flour
2 tbs vinegar
1 can of beer
1 tsp salt
2 tbs mixed herbs

Mix the ingredients together. No kneading needed. No need to wait for it to rise. Put the mixture in a bread tin and cook for 45 minutes. Can be topped with grated cheese or parmesan.

From Mary Mell of Stratton.

AMERICAN CARROT CAKE

2 cups plain flour
1½ cups cooking oil (preferably safflower)
¾ cup chopped walnut pieces
1 tsp ground cloves
1 tsp salt
3 cups grated carrot
2 cups sugar
1 tsp cinnamon
1 tsp baking soda
4 eggs

Beat eggs, sugar and oil in a mixer until creamy and all sugar is dissolved. Add the dry ingredients, walnuts and spices, alternately with the grated carrot. Mix well.

Bake for 1 hour at 170°C in a large round cake tin.

Turn out on tray and when cool, ice with chocolate icing (butter, cocoa and icing sugar — add some rum essence and vanilla). Decorate with walnut pieces, cherries or preserved ginger.

This was given to me by an American lady. It is truly the best.

From E Holly of Kardinya.

R.F.T's CHEESE DAMPER

Firm cheese (parmesan or similar)
1 mug warm milk (same size as flour mug)
1 medium size cake tin or deep baking dish
2 mugs self-raising flour
1 tsp baking powder
½ tsp salt

Pre-heat oven to 200°C and warm a baking tin. (In winter, it also pays to warm the mixing bowl.) Mix flour, baking powder and salt together. Grate in a good serving of cheese and mix again. Make a hole in the middle of the mixture and add warmed milk. Blend together and knead well.

Grease the warmed baking tin with butter and add mixture to centre of tin.

Grate some more cheese over the top then bake for approximately 45 minutes, or until the top goes a crusty brown.

When done, turn out and check underside. If still soft, put back in oven (underside up) for a little while until it is firm.

From Ray Twist of Lesmurdie.

FIVE CUP LOAF

1 cup All-Bran	1 cup self-raising flour
1 cup mixed fruit	1 cup milk
1 cup brown sugar	Sprinkling of walnuts

Soak All-Bran in milk until absorbed. Stir in mixed fruit, brown sugar, flour and then walnuts. Cooked in greased loaf tin at 180°C for 1 hour. It is delicious spread with butter.

From Carlene Davidson of Quindalup.

CHOCOLATE SQUARES

125 gms butter	$1/2$ tsp baking powder
$3/4$ cup sugar	3 tbs milk
$1/2$ cup coconut	1 cup flour
$1/2$ cup cereal crumbs (Weetbix is good)	1 tbs cocoa
1 cup sultanas	

Cream together the butter and sugar. Add coconut, sultanas and cereal crumbs. Add all other ingredients. Bake in 20 cm square tin for 30 minutes at 180°C. Do not overcook. Ice and cut into squares while still warm.

From Hazel Milldove of Beechboro.

Bread is the staff of life.

Jonathan Swift, *Tales of a Tub.*

DAY BEFORE PAYDAY CAKE

1 cup dates	1 tbs butter
2 cups self-raising flour	1 cup boiling water
$3/4$ cup brown sugar	
(white can be used instead but brown is best.)	

Stir the butter, brown sugar, dates and boiling water. Add the self-raising flour and mix. Put the mixture in a cake tin and bake in a moderate oven for about 1 hour. Cake slices can be buttered if you like.

From Mary Masters of Padbury.

FRUIT AND NUT SLICE

125 gms margarine
1 dsp golden syrup
1 cup mixed fruit
1 large cup self-raising flour

1 small cup sugar
1 egg
$1/2$ cup walnuts

Melt margarine, sugar and golden syrup. Allow to cool slightly. Add egg, fruit, nuts and flour. Press into flat tin and bake in a moderate oven for 20 minutes. Cut into squares while warm.

From L Garnett of Myaree.

COCONUT SHORTBREAD

1 cup self-raising flour
1 cup coconut

$1/2$ cup sugar
125 gms margarine, melted

Mix the dry ingredients. Add the melted margarine. Mix well and press into greased Swiss roll tin. Bake in moderate oven until brown. Cool and then ice with chocolate icing. Cut into pieces while warm.

From Dodie Brewer of Floreat.

WHEATGERM LOAF

1 cup wheatgerm
1 cup sultanas or other fruit
$1 1/4$ cups self-raising flour or wholemeal flour

$1/2$ cup sugar
$1 1/2$ cups milk

Soak the wheatgerm, sugar and fruit in the milk for approximately 1 hour. Mix in the flour and combine well.

Place in greased and floured loaf tin. Cook in moderate oven for 45 minutes.

This loaf is lovely with butter. It also freezes very well.

From Pat Beer of Kenwick.

ALL IN TOGETHER CAKE

125 gms margarine (softened)	2 eggs
1 cup caster sugar	1 cup self raising flour
2 heaped tbs custard powder	³/₄ cup milk

Beat all the ingredients together until well combined. Bake at 180°C for approximately 45 minutes.

For variation, add cocoa for chocolate, colouring for marble, or lemon juice and coconut.

From Betty Riley of South Lake.

DIABETIC FRUIT LOAF

100 gms chopped dates	100 gms raisins
100 gms margarine	30 gms chopped walnuts
155 gms self-raising flour	Pinch mixed spices
155 mls boiling water	Pinch baking powder

Put the dates and raisins in a bowl and pour over the boiling water. Leave to soak for 10 minutes. Add the margarine and nuts, then the flour, spice and baking powder. Pour into a greased loaf tin and bake for 1 hour. This can be cut into 10 slices and frozen.

From Margaret Ashworth of South Mandurah.

The smell of buttered toast simply talked to Toad, and with no uncertain voice: talked of warm kitchens, of breakfasts on bright frosty mornings, of cosy parlour firesides on winter evenings, when one's ramble was over and slippered feet were propped on the fender; of the purring of cats, and the twitter of sleepy canaries.

Kenneth Grahame, *The Wind In The Willows.*

LAZY CAKE

1 cup self raising flour
½ cup sugar
2 dsp margarine
1 cup milk
1 egg
2 dsp cocoa

Beat all the ingredients together. Put in a greased pan and cook in a moderate oven for 30 minutes.

From Margaret Ashworth of South Mandurah.

BARA BRITH

400 gms mixed fruit
300 mls hot black tea
500 gms self-raising flour
1 tbs thick cut marmalade
250 gms sugar
60 gms butter
Pinch salt
1 egg, well beaten

Soak mixed fruit, sugar and black tea overnight. Rub butter and flour together with salt, then add the egg. Add the soaked ingredients, marmalade and mix well together.

Grease the loaf tin and set the oven to 180°C. Bake for 1-1½ hours. This recipe is originally from Wales.

From Laurie of Wanneroo.

LEMON CAKE

125 gms margarine
185 gms sugar
Grated rind & juice of 1 lemon
2 eggs
4 tbs milk
185 gms self-raising flour

Cream margarine and sugar. Add lemon rind, eggs and milk. Beat well for 5 minutes. Place in a greased loaf tin on the centre shelf of the oven and cook for approximately 1 hour at 180°C. Mix 3 dessertspoons of icing sugar with lemon juice and spoon over cake when cooked but still in tin — hot. Before turning out, allow 3 to 4 drops of lemon juice to drip into cake.

From Joy Parsons of Morley.

SCONES

4 cups self-raising flour
300 mls water
300 mls carton cream
Pinch salt

Mix everything together lightly and place in rectangular tray. Pat into shape and cut into squares. Glaze tops. Bake in a hot oven for 12-15 minutes.

From Janice of Como.

SWEET IMPOSSIBLE PIE

5 eggs
1/2 cup sugar
1 cup shredded coconut
Orange, pineapple or banana extract
1 tbs butter
1/2 cup plain flour
2 tsp vanilla
1 cup milk

Mix ingredients in order and pour into a 20cm pie pan lightly greased. Bake on 350°C for 40-45 minutes.

The result is a pie crust, custard filling and coconut top.

From Dianne Lannu of Wilson. This recipe was given to her by her 82-year-old dad and was the first Grapevine recipe to be broadcast.

Of all smells, bread; of all tastes, salt.
George Herbert.

ANKE'S DEADLY DATE DELIGHT

250 gms butter
1 pkt Marie biscuits — broken not crushed
250 gm dried dates — washed and chopped
1/2 cup sugar
1 tsp vanilla essence
1 lightly beaten egg

Melt butter and sugar together. As soon as bubbles appear, remove from heat. Add biscuits and stir in remaining ingredients. Pack into tin tray. Refrigerate. When set, cut into small squares and roll in coconut.

From Debbie Jones of Balcatta.

TRIPLE CHOCOLATE MUFFINS

2½ cups self-raising flour
1 cup Choc-Bits
1¾ cups milk
¼ cup icing sugar

½ cup cocoa
90 gms melted butter
125 gms cream cheese
100 gms melted chocolate

Mix together flour, cocoa, Choc-Bits, butter and milk. Grease muffin pans well. Spoon mixture into pans ¾ full into each cup. Bake for 25 minutes at 190°C.

For the icing: mix cream cheese, icing sugar and melted chocolate. Place the icing onto the cool muffins.

From Eileen of Balcatta.

CHOCOLATE CRUNCH

1 cup flour
100 gms butter
1 beaten egg
1 tbs cocoa

1 tsp baking powder
¾ cup sugar
1 tsp vanilla essence
¾ cup desiccated coconut

Melt the butter and add the sugar. Add the beaten egg and vanilla essence. Mix the flour and cocoa together and fold in the coconut. Press onto greased and lined tray. Bake for 20 minutes at 190°C.

From Eileen of Balcatta.

THE PETER-PROOF CHOCOLATE CAKE

1 cup self-raising flour
¾ cup sugar
1 tbs melted butter
1 egg

Pinch salt
2 dsp cocoa
¾ cup milk
1 tsp vanilla essence

Put all ingredients in a bowl and mix for 2 minutes. Pour into a lined tin. Bake for 30 minutes on 180°C, or until cooked. Ice when cold.

From Bea Davies of Hamilton Hill. She says this recipe is so simple, even Peter Holland couldn't mess it up!

Liz says, 'Bea was wrong! Peter did mess it up — but the recipe does make a delicious cake.'

CHILDREN'S CRAZY COOKIES

60 gms butter/margarine
1 pkt Smarties
1 pkt small jubes or other soft lollies
Food colouring (several colours)
1 pkt Milk Arrowroot biscuits or 1 pkt Granita or similar plain biscuits

1 tbs hot water
$\frac{1}{2}$ cup icing sugar
1 pkt licorice

Cream butter and icing sugar until soft and creamy. Add hot water, a little at a time to make a soft paste. Separate into smaller bowls and add a different food colouring to each bowl. Spread the icing mixture onto the plain biscuits. Decorate and make faces using the soft lollies, licorice and Smarties.

From Katharine of Karrinyup.

PICKLES, PRESERVES, BEVERAGES

STRAWBERRY LIQUEUR

1 kg strawberries
200 gms sugar

500 mls Polish Spirit

Slice strawberries as thinly as possible and place in a screw-top jar. Add spirit. Screw top down tightly. Leave in a cupboard for 3 months.

Dissolve sugar in the smallest amount of warm white wine possible. Mix with strawberry mixture and leave a further 3 months.

Drink sparingly after dinner (approximately 40% alcohol), slightly chilled. Be very careful — this is very strong! Don't even think about driving!

From Guy of Perth.

LEMON CORDIAL

Grated rind of 4 lemons
4 cups boiling water
Juice of 4-6 lemons
4 cups sugar

Put sugar and lemon rind into large bowl. Add boiling water and stir until sugar is dissolved. Add lemon juice, strain and bottle. Store in refrigerator.

If kept in the fridge, this cordial will keep for several weeks. Add ice and water before drinking.

From Peg of Shenton Park.

ALMOND MILK

1 cup almonds
2 cups water

Place almonds and water in a blender. Mix thoroughly. Strain mixture through a wire strainer lined with a square of nylon curtain material.

Almond milk can be used in place of dairy or soy milk, but not for cooking.

Lovely for milkshakes.

From Merrill Griechen of Bullsbrook.

GRAN'S CHILLI WINE

3 cups sugar
2 tsp tartaric acid
$1/2$ tsp chillies
3 tsp lemon essence
6 litres boiling water
2 tbs burnt sugar

Mix all ingredients together and let stand for 1 hour. Strain and bottle.

From my grandmother's personal recipe book. She was going to be a missionary before she met Grandpa, so the book also contains improving tracts and moral Victorian quotes.

From Virginia O'Keeffe.

MULLED WINE

Pinch nutmeg
3 tbs brown sugar
Juice and rind of 1 lemon or orange
1 bottle dry red wine (elderberry or blackberry are good, or ordinary table wine)
1 stick cinnamon
3 cloves
$1/2$ pint hot water

Simmer all ingredients, except wine, for 20 minutes. Add wine. Reheat but do not boil. Serve immediately.

Many thanks to all the Grapies who sent us their mulled wine recipes. This one is from Linda Ogden of Parmelia.

GINGER BEER

$5\frac{1}{2}$ litres cold water
Juice 4 lemons
4 cups sugar
2 tbs ginger

Stir all ingredients together until sugar has dissolved. Put into screw-top jars, adding 3-4 sultanas to each jar. Leave for 2-3 days until sultanas have risen. Strain and chill.

This is a recipe my mother used years ago.

From Pat Beer of Kenwick.

THE ULTIMATE SUN-DRIED TOMATO RECIPE

Roma tomatoes
Basil, garlic, sliced chilli, peppercorns
Olive oil

Cut each tomato into 4 wedges. Place on a plastic mesh on a frame, and sprinkle with salt. Cover with a mosquito net, place outside in the sun. (Make sure the frame stand is ant-proof!)

The tomatoes are 'done' when they are dry, but feel slightly rubbery. Rinse in fresh water to remove some of the salt. Re-dry the tomatoes.

Pack tightly in a jar with a scattering of herbs. Fill the jar with olive oil.

From Erica of Kelmscott.

BRINE SOLUTION FOR OLIVES

Ripe olives
1 cup brown vinegar
3 cups water
$1/2$ cup salt

Place olives in jar. Mix water, vinegar and salt. Fill each jar with brine solution, covering olives completely. Put a film of olive oil on the top. Seal airtight for 8 weeks or until sweet.

Wash fruit, add 3 or 4 crushed garlic cloves, 3 or 4 sprigs of rosemary and a teaspoon of dry red wine.

This was sent by an anonymous Grapie and was deemed the easiest olive-preserving recipe ever!

The rule is, jam tomorrow and jam yesterday, but never jam today.

Lewis Carroll, *Through The Looking Glass.*

ZUCCHINI RELISH

500 gms zucchini, chopped
1 stick celery, chopped
1 red capsicum, chopped
1 kg ripe tomatoes, chopped
2 cups sugar
2 tbs flour
$1/4$ cup water
1 tbs curry powder
2 tbs dry mustard
$1 1/2$ cups vinegar

Put all vegetables except tomatoes in a bowl. Sprinkle with salt, cover with water and stand overnight. Drain and rinse.

Put all vegetables including tomatoes in a pan and bring to the boil. Simmer for 10 minutes. Add sugar and stir to dissolve.

Mix curry powder, mustard, flour and water to make a smooth paste. Add carefully to mixture and simmer for 5 minutes.

Bottle in sterilised jars.

From Linda of Ballajura.

OLIVE DIP

2 cups stoneless black olives
Juice of ½ lemon
2 cloves garlic
2 anchovies

Blend all ingredients together and serve. The dip looks a bit like caviar and is best served on fresh, crusty bread. It keeps for ages in the fridge.

I am a Cypriot brought up with olives in all their forms, but I did not discover them in a dip until I visited an Italian restaurant in Beverly Hills.

From Theo Zavros of Kallaroo.

PAPRIKA SAUCE

6 tbs pineapple juice
6 tbs lemon juice
3 eggs, lightly beaten
90 gms sugar
Pinch salt
1 level tsp paprika

Place all ingredients in the top of a double saucepan. Stir until sauce thickens. Serve with sliced fresh fruit.

This unusual recipe was given to me years ago by my friend Kaye, in Melbourne. It is always popular.

From Judith Montgomerie of Shenton Park.

JEWISH-STYLE PICKLED CUCUMBERS

1 kg Lebanese cucumbers
½ pkt fresh dill or 1 tsp dill seeds
1 tsp fresh chopped chilli (include seeds)
Salt solution: 1 tbs salt/1 cup water
6 grapevine leaves
5 cloves garlic
6 bay leaves

Pack cucumbers in a screw-top jar. Arrange grapevine leaves between the cucumbers and add the rest of the ingredients. Seal jars and place in a sunny, subdued spot until they turn yellowish (about 3-4 days). Store in a cool cupboard.

They will be ready to enjoy after 14 days. Refrigerate after opening.

From D Sykes of Alfred Cove.

CAULIFLOWER PICKLE

1 large cauliflower	1½ cups cooking salt
2 litres vinegar	2 tbs mustard
1 cup plain flour	750 gms onions
1 tbs turmeric	4 cups sugar

Cut cauliflower into sections and put into a pan of boiling water. Add the salt, boil for 1 minute then strain. Boil the onions in 3 cups of vinegar.

Mix mustard, turmeric, flour and sugar together and blend with remaining cup of cold vinegar. Make a smooth paste. Add to the boiling vinegar and onions.

Boil for 1 minute. Add drained cauliflower and bring back to the boil, stirring occasionally to prevent sticking. Remove from heat and bottle. It will fill 7 pickle jars.

From Mrs J McNamara of Westfield.

Lady at a dinner party: 'You mean to tell me that you never, ever let water touch your lips? Then what do you use to clean your teeth, pray?'
Retired major: 'A light Sauterne, madam.'

Anon.

CHILLI CHUTNEY

1 cup chopped chillies, seeded	1 cup chopped raisins
1 cup chopped green apples	1 cup brown sugar
1 cup chopped onions	1 cup brown vinegar

Put all ingredients in a saucepan and cook until tender. Thicken with 1 tablespoon of cornflour. Bottle while hot.

From D Dhu of Mandurah.

SEVILLE ORANGE MARMALADE

1½ kg Seville oranges
12 cups sugar, warmed
Juice 2 lemons
14 cups water

Quarter the oranges lengthwise. Remove the seeds and centre pith and tie them in a piece of muslin. Slice the oranges and put in a bowl with the muslin bag and half the water. Leave overnight. Next day, transfer to a saucepan, add the rest of the water and lemon juice and simmer until the fruit is tender and the liquid is reduced by half. Add the sugar, stir until it has dissolved and bring to the boil. Boil rapidly until setting point is reached. Remove from the heat, cool for 10 minutes. Stir gently, pour into warm sterilised jars and seal.

To test for setting: put some marmalade on a cold saucer and wait for 20 seconds. Then run your finger through it to make a crack. If it crinkles at the edges and the track remains, making 2 separate portions, it is ready. Alternatively, spoon a little of the marmalade onto a cold saucer and leave to cool. It will wrinkle when pushed with a finger if setting point has been reached.

Many thanks to the Grapies who sent marmalade recipes. This one is from George Goodey and is taken from the Australian Family Circle Cookbook. *It is reprinted here with kind permission from Murdoch Books.*

'What's Cooking'
with 720 ABC radio

Most fellas say, 'Nothing beats my mother's cooking'. In my case it had to be 'make it fit for human consumption'! So because of this it wasn't until I left home at 18 that I discovered chops did not need to be raw in the middle, vegies need not be boiled to the consistency of paper maché, a salad tasted better with less mayo and more oil and vinegar. And ever since then, food for me has not been survival, but a journey. Still, in all honesty, I've never tasted better than my mum's bread and butter pudding· the only thing she could cook!

Ted Bull.

The thing I love about food is the way it brings people together. Sharing a meal, whether it is a dinner party, a working breakfast or just a chat over coffee and cake, is one of my greatest pleasures. I enjoy good company and conversation, and food seems to enrich the experience. It doesn't always help if you're trying to watch what you eat though ... so I try to teach myself to enjoy a little less and savour it more!

Liz Byrski.

My idea of bliss is an afternoon spent cooking and an evening spent with wonderful, exotic food and wine, a group of close (or not so close) friends and talking 'til early in the morning. I'm just waiting for the first time my children, Maddie and Isobella, join the fray. They're past the 'throwing the food about the walls' stage, but not quite into fine food appreciation. That, I think, will be really delightful.

Fiona Guthrie.

While I'm not particularly distinguished at the preparation end of this food business, I have a great regard for those of you who are, because some of my finest achievements have been at the consumption end of it. May the spirit of the Grapevine inhabit these pages and many happy meals grow from it.

Peter Holland.

Food is so much more than sustenance. It is a playful, passionate love affair, respect for which must be developed and honoured. It is so intricately tied in with our emotional highs and lows. When we celebrate, it's out to dinner with champagne; when we're sad, it's chocolate in all its magnificent forms. When we care, we seek to nurture by preparing comfort food from the heart. Yes I love it. I live it!

Verity James.

How times have changed: and for the better. It wasn't that long ago that spaghetti in particular, and pasta in general, made only rare appearances on our dining tables. A generation later, it's commonplace. Simple to prepare and tasty to boot!

Peter Kennedy.

Breakfast is the most important meal of the day. But watching kids spread sloppy cereal from wall to wall can have such an impact! You can't decide whether to discipline them or just join in. It's a good thing I'm at work.

Michael Schultz.

INDEX

5-Day Soup	14
Abbundanza Soup	12
Almond Milk	86
Anzac Biscuits	75
Apricot Delight	71
Asparagus	
and Smoked Salmon Fettucine	60
and Chicken Casserole	48
Apple and Pumpkin Soup	7
Bacon and Egg Pie	37
Baked Fish	53
Banana Curry Soup	9
Bara Brith	81
Basil Pasta	59
Beef	
5-minute Chilli	42
in Plum Sauce	44
Beer	
Bread	76
Ginger	87
Beverages	
Almond Milk	86
Chilli Wine	86
Ginger Beer	87
Lemon Cordial	86
Mulled Wine	87
Strawberry Liqueur	85
Biscuits	
Anzac Biscuits	75
Children's Crazy Cookies	84
Chocolate Crunch	83
Coconut Shortbread	79
Deadly Date Delight	82
Bread	
Bara Brith	81
Beer	76
Cheese Damper	77
Cheese Muffins	76
Diabetic Fruit Loaf	80
Five Cup Loaf	78
Lemonade Scones	76
Scones	82
Triple Chocolate Muffins	83

Wheatgerm Loaf	79
Butternut Pumpkin Microwave Soup	9
Cabbage	
Garlic	27
Swedish spiced red	36
Soup	12
Caesar	
Potato Salad	23
Salad, Definitive	21
Cakes	
All In Together	80
American Carrot	77
Chocolate	83
Chocolate Squares	78
Day Before Payday	78
Fruit and Nut Slice	79
Lazy	81
Lemon	81
Sweet Impossible Pie	82
Caldo Verdi	8
Camembert, Deep Fried	27
Capsicums, roasted red	33
Carrot	
and Cauliflower Soup	8
Coriander Soup	11
Cake, American	77
Cauliflower	
and Carrot Soup	8
Pickle	90
Cheese	
Damper	77
Muffins	76
Sticks	29
Cheesey Egg	29
Chicken	
and Corn Soup, Chinese	10
Rice Soup, Thai with Coriander	17
Asparagus Casserole	48
Baked in Barbecue Sauce	46
Chilli Salad	23
Greek	45
Green Casserole	49
in Coke	46

in Orange	45
Mushroom Fillets	49
Renoir	47
Roast Italian Style	47
Simple Simon	48
Spaghetti	58
Surprise	42
Chilli	
Beef, 5-minute	42
Chicken Salad	23
Chutney	90
Con Carne	32
Wine	86
Chocolate	
Cake	83
Crunch	83
Muffins, Triple	83
Squares	78
Chutney, Chilli	90
Coconut Shortbread	79
Compost Soup	8
Copper Penny Salad	19
Cordial, Lemon	86
Coriander and Carrot Soup	11
Corn	
and Chicken Soup, Chinese	10
Fritters, curried with minted sour cream	31
Corned Beef Hash	39
Crab Quiche	53
Creamy Pasta Sauce, Healthy	60
Cucumbers, Pickled Jewish-style	89
Curry Sauce, cold for Chicken	48
Date Delight	82
Desserts	
Apricot Delight	71
Eggless Plum Pudding	73
Fruit Jelly	70
Fruit Salad	68
Fudge	67
Golden Puffs	71
Golden Syrup Pudding	74
Mango Mousse	68
Pancakes	69
Passionfruit Jelly	69
Pineapple Marshmallow	69
Pineapple Surprise	70
Pineapple Tidbits	67
Queen of Puddings	72
Quick Peach	67

Raspberry/Loganberry Mush	70
Rum Plums	68
Russian Cream	71
Show Me Pudding	73
Sligo Pudding	66
Treacle Pudding	72

Dressings
- Herb Vinaigrette — 25
- Mayonnaise — 25
- Minted sour cream — 31
- Sour Cream — 25

Egg
- and Bacon Pie — 37
- Cheesey — 29
- Soup — 11

Eggbake, Breakfast — 28
Fettucine with Asparagus and Smoked Salmon — 60
Figs and Prosciutto — 38
Filo Pastry Meat and Vegetable Parcels — 43

Fish
- Baked Fish — 53
- Crunchy Tuna Rolls — 54
- Fillet de Gummy Shark aux Herbes — 52
- Fish Minestrone — 52
- Fish Mornay — 51
- Fish Patties — 55
- Mock Schnapper — 55
- Smoked Mackerel Paté — 54
- Tuna and Tomato Dip — 56
- Tuna Casserole — 55

Fruit
- and Nut Slice — 79
- Jelly — 70
- Loaf, Diabetic — 80
- Salad Dessert — 68

Fudge — 67
Garlic Cabbage — 27
Ginger Beer — 87
Gnocchi with Gorgonzola Sauce — 58
Golden Syrup Pudding — 74
Greek Chicken — 45
Green Soup — 13
Gummy Shark, aux Herbes — 52
Herb Vinaigrette — 25

Jelly
- Fruit — 70
- Passionfruit — 69

JMs Savoury — 29

Lamb
    and Potato Soup   13
    Roast with Redcurrant Sauce   43
Lasagne
    Spinach   64
    Tuna   63
    Vegetarian   30
Lemon
    Cake   81
    Cordial   86
Lemonade Scones   76
Lentil Soup   15
Lettuce Soup   15
Loganberry Mush   70
Mackerel Paté, Smoked   54
Mango Mousse   68
Marmalade, Seville Orange   91
Marshmallow
    Salad   24
    Pineapple Dessert   69
Mayonnaise   25
Meat
    5-minute Chilli Beef   42
    A La Bullers   39
    A Meal in a Pot   45
    Beef in Plum Sauce   44
    Corned Beef Hash   39
    Egg and Bacon Pie   37
    Figs and Prosciutto   38
    Filo Pastry Meat and Vegetable Parcels   43
    Lamb Roast with Redcurrant Sauce   43
    Lecso   46
    Meat Loaf   39
    Pork Chops, fruited   40
    Pork Casserole   41
    Salamugundy   42
    Sausage Curry   40
    Sausage Stew   38
    Sausage Stroganoff   44
    Veal Oregano   41
Mediterranean Pasta Salad   20
Mexican Rice   65
Milk, Almond   86
Mozzarella Napolitana   62
Muffins, Cheese   76
Mulled Wine   87
Mushroom Chicken Fillets   49
Mustard and Pumpkin Salad   18
Nasturtium Leaves, stuffed   35

Noodle Salad	22
Nut Slice, Fruit and	79
Orange Marmalade, Seville	91
Pancakes	69
Pan Haggerty	26
Paprika Sauce	89
Parsley Pesto	35
Passionfruit Jelly	69
Pasta	
Atlantic College Spaghetti	59
Basil Pasta	59
Chicken Spaghetti	58
Creamy Pasta Sauce	60
Fettucine with Asparagus and Smoked Salmon	60
Gnocchi with Gorgonzola Sauce	58
Mozzarella Napolitana	62
Pasta All'amatriciana	57
Pasta Hotch-Potch	61
Pasta Y.E.S	61
Peak Hill Pasta Sauce	62
Spinach Lasagne	64
Spinach Pasta	59
Tomato Sauce, Easy for Pasta or Pizza	58
Tuna Lasagne	63
Pasta Salad, Mediterranean	20
Peach Dessert, Quick	67
Pesto, Parsley	35
Pickles	
Brine for Olives	88
Cauliflower	90
Chilli Chutney	90
Cucumbers, Jewish-Style	89
Olive Dip	89
Zucchini Relish	88
Pineapple	
Marshmallow Dessert	69
Surprise	70
Tidbits	67
Plum Pudding, Eggless	73
Plums, Rum	68
Polenta, grilled	34
Pork	
Casserole	41
Chops, fruited	40
Potato	
and Lamb Soup	13
Rounds	27
Salad, Caesar	23

Poultry
- Asparagus Chicken Casserole — 48
- Chicken Baked in Barbecue Sauce — 46
- Chicken, Cold Curry Sauce for — 48
- Chicken in Coke — 46
- Chicken in Orange — 45
- Chicken Mushroom Fillets — 49
- Chicken Surprise — 42
- Greek Chicken — 45
- Green Casserole Chicken — 49
- Renoir Chicken — 47
- Roast Chicken Italian Style — 47
- Simple Simon Chicken — 48

Prawns, Curried — 50

Preserves
- Seville Orange Marmalade — 91

Prosciutto and Figs — 38

Pumpkin
- and Apple Soup — 7
- and Mustard Salad — 18

Queen of Puddings — 72

Quiche
- Crab — 53
- Impossible — 30

Raspberry Mush — 70

Rice
- Mexican Rice — 65
- Savoury Rice Casserole — 63
- Spinach — 63
- Tomato Risotto — 64

Rice and Chicken Soup, Thai with Coriander — 17
Risotto, Tomato — 64
Rockmelon Soup, chilled — 16
Rum Plums — 68
Russian Cream — 71

Salads
- Caesar, Definitive — 21
- Caesar, Potato — 23
- Chilli Chicken — 23
- Copper Penny — 19
- Marshmallow — 24
- Mediterranean Pasta — 20
- Noodle — 22
- Pumpkin and Mustard — 18
- Seafood — 22
- Silverbeet — 19
- Silverbeet No 2 — 20
- Spinach — 18
- Summer — 19

Summer, Quick	21
Tuna, Continental	24
Salamugundy	42
Sausage	
Curry	40
Stew	38
Stroganoff	44
Savoury Rice Casserole	63
Scallops, Quick	53
Schnapper, Mock	55
Scones	82
Scones, Lemonade	76
Seafood	
Crab Quiche	53
Curried Prawns	50
Quick Scallops	53
Sloshed Squid	50
and Tomato Soup	16
Salad	22
Sesame Burgers	31
Seville Orange Marmalade	91
Shannon, cold	14
Shortbread, Coconut	79
Silverbeet	
Salad	19
Salad No 2	20
Sligo Pudding	66
Smoked Mackerel Paté	54
Smoked Salmon and Asparagus Fettucine	60
Soup	
5-Day	14
Abbundanza	12
Apple and Pumpkin	7
Banana Curry Soup	9
Butternut Pumpkin Microwave Soup	9
Cabbage	12
Caldo Verde	8
Carrot and Cauliflower	8
Carrot and Coriander	11
Chicken and Corn, Chinese	10
Compost	8
Egg	11
Green	13
Lentil	15
Lettuce	15
Potato and Lamb	13
Rockmelon	16
Shannon, cold	14
Summer	16

Thai Chicken and Rice	17
Tomato and Seafood	16
Tomato and Yoghurt	15
Vichyssoise	10
Wild Rice and Spinach	10
Sour Cream Dressing	25
Spaghetti	
Atlantic College	59
Chicken	58
Spinach	
and Wild Rice Soup	10
Lasagne	64
Pasta	59
Salad	18
Rice	63
Rolls	33
Squid, Sloshed	50
Strawberry Liqueur	85
Summer	
Salad	19
Salad, Quick	21
Soup	16
Tomato	
Seafood Soup	16
Tuna Dip	56
Yoghurt Soup	15
Risotto	64
Sauce, Easy for Pasta or Pizza	58
Sun-dried	87
Treacle Pudding	72
Tuna	
and Tomato Dip	56
Casserole	55
Lasagne	63
Rolls, Crunchy	54
Salad, Continental	24
Veal Oregano	41
Vegetables, baked	28
Vegetarian Dishes	
Breakfast Eggbake	28
Camembert, Deep Fried	27
Cheese Sticks	29
Cheesey Egg	29
Chilli Con Carne	32
Corn Fritters, curried, with minted sour cream	31
Garlic Cabbage	27
JMs Savoury	29
Nasturtium Leaves, stuffed	35
Pan Haggerty	26

Parsley Pesto	35
Polenta, grilled	34
Potato Rounds	27
Quiche, Impossible	30
Red Cabbage, Swedish spiced	36
Red Capsicums, roasted	33
Sesame Burgers	31
Spinach Rolls	33
Vegetables, baked	28
Vegetarian Lasagne	30
Zucchini Slice	34
Vegetarian Lasagne	30
Vichyssoise	10
Vinaigrette, Herb	25
Wheatgerm Loaf	79
Wild Rice and Spinach Soup	10
Wine	
Chilli	86
Mulled	87
Yoghurt and Tomato Soup	15
Zucchini	
Relish	88
Slice	34